Transpersonal
Communication

Transpersonal Books
JAMES FADIMAN, *General Editor*

Transpersonal Books
explore the psychology of consciousness,
and possibilities for transcendence
through altered states of consciousness,
paranormal phenomena, spiritual disciplines,
and other modes of extended awareness.

BOOKS IN THE SERIES

Barry K. Weinhold is professor of counselor education at the University of Colorado, Colorado Springs.

Lynn C. Elliott is a counselor/supervisor at Gemini House, a residential facility for abused adolescents in Wheat Ridge, Colorado.

Transpersonal Communication

How to Establish Contact with Yourself and Others

BARRY K. WEINHOLD
LYNN C. ELLIOTT

A SPECTRUM BOOK

PRENTICE-HALL, INC., Englewood Cliffs, N.J. 07632

Library of Congress Cataloging in Publication Data

Weinhold, Barry K
   Transpersonal communication.

   (Transpersonal books) (A Spectrum Book)
   Bibliography: p.
   Includes index.
   1. Interpersonal communication. 2. Self-perception.
I. Elliott, Lynn C., joint author. II. Title.
BF637.C45W375   158'.2   79–10871
ISBN 0–13–930396–0
ISBN 0–13–930388–X pbk.

© 1979 by Barry K. Weinhold & Lynn C. Elliott

A SPECTRUM BOOK

10 9 8 7 6 5 4 3 2 1

Printed in the United States of America

Editorial/production supervision and interior
design by Norma Miller Karlin
Cover design by Ira Shapiro
Manufacturing buyer: Cathie Lenard

PRENTICE-HALL INTERNATIONAL, INC., *London*
PRENTICE-HALL OF AUSTRALIA PTY. LIMITED, *Sydney*
PRENTICE-HALL OF CANADA, LTD., *Toronto*
PRENTICE-HALL OF INDIA PRIVATE LIMITED, *New Delhi*
PRENTICE-HALL OF JAPAN, INC., *Tokyo*
PRENTICE-HALL OF SOUTHEAST ASIA PTE. LTD., *Singapore*
WHITEHALL BOOKS LIMITED, *Wellington, New Zealand*

Contents

Contents

3

THE MAGIC CARPET RIDE IN THE CLASSROOM 28

4

THE DAY YOU TALKED TO YOURSELF
AND SOMEONE ANSWERED 34

5

HOW TO INTEGRATE INTRAPERSONAL
COMMUNICATION SKILLS
INTO THE REGULAR CURRICULUM 40

II

INTERPERSONAL COMMUNICATION SKILLS 45

6

STOP, LOOK, AND LISTEN 49

7

STRAIGHTENING OUT THE MAZE 69

8

BECOMING REAL 77

9

MY VALUES ARE BETTER THAN YOURS 84

10

TEACHER, MAY I? 88

Contents

II
PARDON MY RELATIONSHIPS

I2
HOW TO INTEGRATE INTERPERSONAL
COMMUNICATION SKILLS
INTO THE REGULAR CURRICULUM

III
TRANSPERSONAL SKILLS IN COMMUNICATION

I3
BELOW YOUR NAVEL

I4
HIGH ENERGY: ACTIVITIES IN ENERGY AWARENESS

I5
IT'S ONLY YOUR IMAGINATION

I6
RIDING THE COSMIC ROLLER COASTER

I7
JOURNEY BEYOND THE SELF

I8
THE COLLECTIVE SELF
AND THE MYTH OF ALONENESS

Contents

19

HOW TO INTEGRATE TRANSPERSONAL
COMMUNICATION SKILLS
INTO THE REGULAR CURRICULUM   178

IV

HOLISTIC PERSPECTIVES IN EDUCATION   189

20

THE TRANSPERSONAL TEACHER   191

21

TEACHING AS TRANSPERSONAL COMMUNICATION   201

V

A PARENTS' GUIDE
TO TRANSPERSONAL COMMUNICATION   213

22

TRANSPERSONAL COMMUNICATION AT HOME   215

23

SUGGESTIONS FOR INTRODUCING TRANSPERSONAL
COMMUNICATION IN YOUR SCHOOL DISTRICT   219

List of Activities

Suggestions on How to Use this Book

FOR TEACHERS

We suggest that you read or at least familiarize yourself with the entire book before beginning to integrate the material and activities into your classroom. This step will provide a more thorough understanding of the material, allowing you to choose what you want to use or to modify activities according to the needs of your students.

For training and practice in using the activities in this book, we suggest you first try them out on yourself or with groups of friends or co-workers. This practice will give you the experience necessary to know how to modify the activities for your particular classroom.

If you plan to use most or all of the activities in this book, you may want to have your students divided into small groups of six to eight students for a semester or the school year. These groups can become support groups for students and will help develop trust and closeness with other students.

You will probably have the most success in using this material if you have the support of your school administrators and the students' parents. We suggest that you discuss your plans to integrate the material into the curriculum you teach with your administrators and supervisors. Have occasional "open houses," when parents are invited to visit the classroom, or present your program at P.T.A. meetings to help involve parents. You may also want to enlist interested parents as classroom aides; suggest that they read this book.

Encourage parents and students to use at home the ideas, concepts, and skills presented in this book. The more practice students have, the more skilled they will become, and the more thoroughly they will integrate new learning. Your job will be made easier and the students' families will benefit, too.

We encourage you to read and use other recently published books designed to enrich the children's awareness and capacities;

> *The Centering Book*, by Gay Hendricks and Russel Wills
>
> *The Second Centering Book*, by Gay Hendricks and Thomas B. Roberts
>
> *Values Clarification*, by Sidney Simon, Leland Howe, and Howard Kirschenbaum
>
> *Transpersonal Education*, edited by Gay Hendricks and James Fadiman
>
> *Everybody's A Winner: A Kid's Guide to New Sports and Fitness*, by Tom Schneider
>
> *Caring, Feeling and Touching*, by Sidney Simon
>
> *Be a Frog, a Bud or a Tree*, by Rachel Carr
>
> *A Peaceable Classroom: Activities to Calm and Free Student Energies*, by Merrill Harmin and Saville Sax
>
> *The Magical Child*, by Joseph Chilton Pearce

We suggest that you read or at least familiarize yourself with the entire book before you begin to use the activities.

Unless you have used similar activities with children before, we encourage you to try the activities yourself or with a group of friends or co-workers. This practice will allow you to be familiar with the activities and give you a chance to identify how you may want to modify or expand them to fit your own style.

The activities and material in this book will be most effective if presented in a sequential fashion to an on-going group of children (or adults). However, many of the activities can be done with individuals.

Your success in using this material will be maximized if you involve the students' teachers and parents. If you have a consulting role in a school, you may wish to present this material to teachers in a series of workshops. You could offer similar workshops for parents as part of training in parenting. This material, which can easily be incorporated into family counseling, can help ease problems in communication and facilitate the resolution of conflict among family members.

You may be in a position to support teachers and help them "sell" the use of this material in the classroom to school administrators.

If you find yourself in the position of hearing student complaints about teachers, the material on interpersonal communications can be useful in facilitating problemsolving.

FOR PARENTS

Section V is specifically written to offer you suggestions and guidelines for integrating this material into your interactions with children. We suggest you read the entire book before beginning so that you thoroughly understand the material.

Although you may not wish to use the activities with your children, we believe you will find the material informative and helpful. We would especially like to call your attention to Section II on interpersonal communication. This section includes specific guidelines and skills and problem-solving strategies useful at home, as well as in any social setting.

You can enhance the environment of your children's schools and improve the quality of learning by introducing training in awareness and communication skills to teachers, school administrators, and school boards. Chapter 23 offers specific suggestions.

We encourage you to read and become familiar with other recently published books that discuss effective parenting and awareness and communication skills:

Raising Kids OK, by Dorothy Babcock and Terry Keepers
The Centering Book, by Gay Hendricks and Russel Wills
The Second Centering Book, by Gay Hendricks and Thomas B. Roberts
Caring, Feeling and Touching, by Sidney Simon

Values Clarification, by Sidney B. Simon, Leland W. Howe, and Howard Kirschenbaum

Transpersonal Education, edited by Gay Hendricks and James Fadiman

Sensory Awareness: The Rediscovery of Experiencing, by Charles Brooks

Parent Effectiveness Training, by Thomas Gordon

Preface

This book represents our attempt to create the broadest possible context for employing effective communication skills in schools and families. It is our belief that if effective interpersonal, intrapersonal, and transpersonal communication skills were integrated into the daily activities of schools and families, it would create healthy climates where everyone could win.

In order to make it possible to teach and learn these skills, we organized the best information and skills we could find in each of three main areas of communication: intrapersonal, interpersonal, and transpersonal. Much has been said about what is wrong with schools and families; this book focuses instead on providing tools to make them better. We designed over sixty activities for you to use with yourself and others. In addition, we provide numerous examples of how you can integrate these skills into traditional subject matter areas. Thus, the book is a practical, action-oriented resource that you can begin using immediately.

One final note. We provide a sort of map that you can use to learn these skills. We are aware that the map is not the territory. There are other communication skills not mentioned; in the area of transpersonal communication we are just starting to map the territory and help us all to understand the nature of human communication more fully.

Transpersonal
Communication

Introduction:
What Is
Transpersonal
Communication?

DEFINITION OF
TRANSPERSONAL COMMUNICATION

Transpersonal communication involves the use of skills and understanding to help you become aware of your essential unity and connectedness with all life energy. It is based upon the belief that unity, not separateness or aloneness, is the basic human condition.

Transpersonal communication rests upon the foundation of effective interpersonal and intrapersonal communication to bring you to an expanded contact with the full range of human experiences in yourself and others. Effective interpersonal communication helps build an atmosphere of trust and connectedness with other people. Effective intrapersonal communication enables you to establish contact with and utilize your inner thoughts, feelings, and experiences. When you have developed the inner and outer trust and contact you are truly free to explore your being at the highest levels.

Transpersonal communication is designed to help you learn to trust the validity of your personal experiences and accept what you learn from them as your best source of wisdom and truth. Including the processes of both thinking and feeling, it teaches you to play hunches, use your

Figure 1. Structure of Transpersonal Communication

intuition, and follow your thoughts and feelings rather than direct them in predetermined ways.

Trust in the validity of personal experiences inevitably will lead you to an affirmation of the inner core of your being that transcends the cultural roles and ego, muscular, and emotional defenses (see Figure 2). This inner core is where your unity with all life energy occurs.

All the many approaches to effective interpersonal and intrapersonal communications can be used creatively in this expanded search for truth

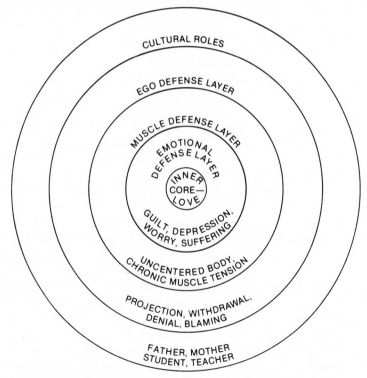

Figure 2. Blocks to Love—Levels of Self-Knowledge

and meaning. Many of the methods developed for humanistic education can be used as a means toward these ends.

THE TRANSPERSONAL SELF

An important goal of transpersonal communication is not to develop a new form of communication in place of existing forms but instead to expand existing forms to include those aspects of human functioning that have been somewhat neglected.

One of the processes of transpersonal communication is the harmony of opposites, that is, bringing harmony and balance to seemingly incompatible aspects of the personality. This process helps you focus on unity rather than separateness so that seemingly opposite concepts—like interpersonal and intrapersonal, higher and lower self, objective and subjective—can be harmonized. The harmony that is established when the conflict of opposites is resolved is expressed in the creation of the *transpersonal self*. This inner core becomes the center of your being and replaces the ego, which now is seen as only a part of being and not the center. In the usual view, the ego is seen as the center of our personality; but this broader view of human functioning is necessary if we are ever going to achieve a balance between intellectual and affective, conscious and unconscious, verbal and nonverbal, and among physical, emotional, mental, and spiritual processes. Figure 3 depicts the transpersonal self.

TRANSPERSONAL COMMUNICATION IN SCHOOLS

Almost everyone agrees that our schools are having trouble keeping up with the rapid changes in our world. What is needed is a new foundation for education, one that is broad enough to include the expanding knowledge and yet teaches us how to get along with ourselves and each other in a rapidly shrinking world.

We believe if transpersonal communication were an integral part of our schools, it would transform the way we educate our children. It could

3

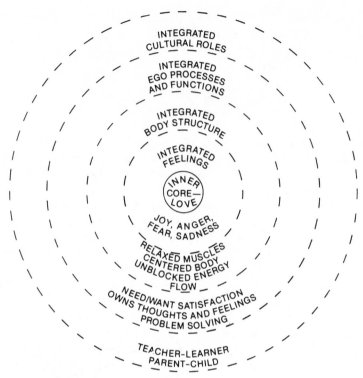

INTEGRATED
CULTURAL ROLES

INTEGRATED
EGO PROCESSES
AND FUNCTIONS

INTEGRATED
BODY STRUCTURE

INTEGRATED
FEELINGS

INNER
CORE—
LOVE

JOY, ANGER,
FEAR, SADNESS

RELAXED MUSCLES
CENTERED BODY
UNBLOCKED ENERGY
FLOW

NEED/WANT SATISFACTION
OWNS THOUGHTS AND FEELINGS
PROBLEM SOLVING

TEACHER-LEARNER
PARENT-CHILD

Figure 3. The Transpersonal Self

provide the foundation for a new educational process that could carry us well into the twenty-first century.

This book will give you a practical, how-to-do-it look at the elements of transpersonal communication and a number of concrete examples of how to integrate its principles into the regular school curriculum. Because we realize that schools will not be transformed over night, most of what we have written in this book can be used in schools as they now exist. The communication skills can be used by teachers, counselors, and administrators in their daily interactions with each other and with their students. The curriculum-related activities we have developed don't require the elimination of an existing curriculum, only its expansion by the integration of these skills and concepts.

4

I

INTRAPERSONAL COMMUNICATION SKILLS

ESSENTIAL INTRAPERSONAL
COMMUNICATION PROCESSES

Your ability to figure out and stay in touch with what is happening inside yourself is referred to as intrapersonal communication. Another term for this process is self-awareness: how aware you are of what is going on inside of you; how you are responding and relating to what is going on outside of you. "Self-reflection is a gazing at one's life and circumstances as though it were a painting to be examined, felt, appreciated. In self-reflection the third or inner eye is opened and one gazes at one's life to learn, appraise, decide."[1]

Self-awareness and the degree to which you are in touch with yourself, your body, and your feelings, thoughts, intuitions, and behavior affects every aspect of your life. Your physical well-being depends upon your awareness of feelings of hunger, tiredness, discomfort, temperature, illness, etc. to give you the information or signals you need to keep yourself in good health. Also, you must be aware of your

---

[1]Wilson Van Dusen, *The Natural Depth in Man* (New York: Harper & Row, Publishers, Inc., 1972), p. 16.

feelings, emotional reactions, wants, and needs in order to act in ways that promote emotional health.

The effectiveness of intrapersonal communication also has a great deal to do with your relationships with others, with interpersonal communication. For instance, if you are feeling tired and irritable but are not aware of it, you may overreact to your friend's request for help and respond angrily, instead of reporting that you are tired and need rest. In fact, unless you are in touch with yourself, you cannot engage in a meaningful, intimate relationship with another person. Self-awareness provides the basis from which other relationships are built. If your awareness of yourself is shallow and incomplete, your relationships with others are likely to be shallow and incomplete also. On the other hand, if you put time and energy into developing personal awareness, you are better able to interact honestly and fully with others.

We have identified the following essential intrapersonal processes which are discussed in this section:

1. awareness of internal sensations, including body awareness, breathing, tension
2. awareness of feelings
3. awareness of thoughts
4. awareness of wants and needs
5. here and now awareness
6. awareness of past influences
7. awareness of unfinished business
8. awareness of dreams and fantasies
9. intuitive processes
10. intrapersonal problem solving

I

The Art
of Talking to Yourself

BECOMING AWARE OF INTERNAL SENSATIONS

The body is constantly sending out signals which can tell you a great deal about yourself if you learn to listen and understand them. Although much is yet to be learned about how we can control bodily functions, biofeedback is being used to help people decrease tension and anxiety, to increase or decrease particular brain waves, to cure migraine headaches and other bodily ills. However, even without the use of fancy equipment, you can learn much about yourself by listening to your body.

BREATHING ON AUTOMATIC

Breathing is one of the most automatic and fundamental functions of the human body. The way that you breathe effects how you feel, how well you think, how much energy you have, and how comfortable you are. Yet, you may not pay attention to your breathing and thus deprive yourself of an important source of information as well as decrease your ability to have positive control over yourself. When I am scared or anxious, my breathing normally becomes rapid and shallow. Continuing to breathe in that manner maintains or increases my feeling of fear. By slowing down my rate of breathing and breathing deeply, it is possible for me to become relaxed.

Tune into your breathing right now. Is it shallow or deep, rapid or slow? Do you breathe into your chest or your stomach?

YOU AND YOUR TENSION

Muscular tension often reflects how you are feeling emotionally, and like breathing, is a source of self-information. It can also be used to either increase or decrease discomfort or a particular state of feeling. Tension in the neck and shoulders is often caused by carrying your head forward or by hunching your shoulders, a bodily stance that often reflects wariness or fear. Such tension can become chronic and therefore go unnoticed, and as long as it is maintained, you cannot be truly relaxed. Also, such chronic tension becomes the repository or storing place for certain feelings and creates emotional blocks in your body. Body techniques, such as rolfing, which is a technique of deep body manipulation, is designed to relieve muscular tension, to realign the body, and release stored up emotions.

By tuning into your body, you can become aware of tensions, which can help you be more aware of your feelings and thoughts. You may sometimes get so involved in doing something that you do not really stay in touch with what you are thinking and feeling. Being alert to body signals can help you recognize how you are feeling and what you are thinking at any given time. You can learn to use this information to increase your self-control, because once you are aware of a particular tension, you can focus attention on the tense area and relax the muscles involved.

As you are reading this, what bodily tensions do you become aware of? Now that you are aware of it, are you usually tense in that area? When do you become tense there?

HOW TO TEACH PEOPLE TO LISTEN
TO THEIR BODIES

ACTIVITY 1—BREATHING

Rationale: Complete breathing involves three motions. Each breath should begin in the abdomen, move up into the middle section of the body, or stomach, and finally, fill the upper chest and collarbone region.

Such breathing is not only invigorating, but also exercises muscles and helps tone the digestive, excretory, and reproductive systems.

Step 1: Have children lie flat on their backs, arms at sides, legs straight. Ask them to pay attention to how they are breathing. Are they only using their upper lungs? Is their breath fast or slow?

Step 2: Now, have them place their right hands on their abdomens and their left hands on their chests. Instruct them to breathe first into their right hands, making them rise, then making their left hands rise. Have them exhale in the same order, making sure their right hands go down first and then their left hands.

To the Teacher: This exercise can be practiced for a few minutes daily. Such breathing exercises also have a calming effect and are a good way to help children make the transition from one activity to another.

Children may also be taught to take a few deep breaths when they are angry or upset, which is useful in helping them learn to think before they act. After they have practiced breathing fully while lying down, they can learn to breathe correctly while sitting or standing.

ACTIVITY 2—TENSION AWARENESS

Rationale: At first, many people have difficulty becoming aware of tension because it is chronic. Thus, it is useful to have people practice or experience exaggerated tension and then relax completely.

Step 1: Have children lie comfortably on their backs, hands at sides, legs straight. Instruct them to take several deep breaths.

Step 2: Instruct them to first tense their muscles for a few seconds and then to relax completely. Begin at their feet and move up through the legs, abdomen, stomach, hands, arms, shoulders, neck, back, and face, first tensing and then relaxing.

Step 3: A variation of this exercise is to have them tense their entire body for a few seconds and then relax.

To the Teacher: This exercise, like the breathing exercise, has a calming effect on children. After practicing both exercises several times, you can help children be more aware of their bodies simply by asking, "How are you breathing right now?" "Where are you tense?" These questions can be asked periodically throughout the day.

To help children understand the connection between body and mind, you can have discussions with them about how they breathe and what muscles they tense in certain situations. Sample discussion questions might be, "When your parents get angry at you, how do you breathe?" "Do you tense certain muscles?" "How do you breathe when you are scared?"

HOW TO TEACH PEOPLE TO STAY
IN TOUCH WITH FEELINGS

ACTIVITY 3—AWARENESS OF FEELINGS

Rationale: Our ability to feel emotionally is related to how well we breathe and to how tense or relaxed we are. Feelings are a very basic level of awareness and are, essentially, a form of energy we can use to think and act more effectively.

As children, many of us are taught that some feelings are not O.K. In order to not feel, we tense a certain part of our bodies, which eventually becomes chronic tension and creates a block to feeling. For instance, if you decide that it isn't O.K. to be sad or to cry, you will shut down your chest area and perhaps tense your face. As you do this, your breathing will become constricted. Because you are stopping yourself from feeling sad, you store sad feelings in those areas of muscular tension. The results are that you may greatly decrease or completely inhibit sad feelings, you decrease your ability to be aware that you are sad, and generally, you impair the healthy functioning of your body and mind.

Feelings are a direct experience of reality and provide you with important information about yourself, what you want and need, what you dislike and like, and how you need to behave to take care of yourself. Without access to the information feelings give you, you will find it hard to be an integrated human being and your effectiveness in all areas of your life will probably be diminished.

In the process of becoming aware of feelings, it is useful to define them and decide what they mean. It is also useful to limit the number of "feeling words" you use so that you and others are clear about what feeling you mean. You can obscure communication and confuse yourself by using many different terms.

Many people find it helpful to use the following five basic feelings and their definitions:

1. Anger—the feeling you have when you do not get what you want or need.
2. Scared—the feeling you have when you anticipate that you won't get what you want or need, or when you lack the information you need to solve a problem.
3. Sad—the feeling you have when you lose somebody or something, as when someone dies.
4. Happy—the feeling you have when you get what you want or need or when you do something effectively.
5. Excited—the feeling you have when you anticipate something good or pleasant.

Step 1: Ask the children to think of as many feeling words as they can and list these on the blackboard, for example, disappointed, upset, depressed, uptight, bummed out, etc. When you have a list of at least twenty-five words, ask the children to see if some of them mean the same thing or have something in common. Suggest that perhaps you can come up with a list of just a few main feelings. Help them identify the five listed above.

Step 2: List the five basic feelings on one side of the board and ask the children to group the other feeling words under these. Some of their words may be a combination of the main feelings. For instance, they may decide that "disappointed" is a combination of "sad" and "angry."

Step 3: Next, ask them to try to define the main feelings: "When do you feel scared; in what situations?" "When do you feel angry?" etc. Try to get a consensus on the definitions and guide the children toward arriving at the definitions listed above.

Step 4: Next, ask the children to think about where they feel the different feelings in their bodies. Discuss such things as the release of adrenalin. List their responses on the board.

Step 5: Discuss what they do with their feelings. A way to approach this step is to ask, "If angry is the feeling we have when we don't get what we want or need, what can we do with that anger so as not to hurt ourselves or others?" Sample answers might be: "Try to get what we want some other way." "Think of something else we want." "Release the anger by shouting or hitting a punching bag." Stress the idea that feelings can be used as a form of energy to help solve problems. Discuss what happens if the children don't express their feelings. Do those feelings build up? What happens in their bodies when they store feelings?

To the Teacher: A number of discussions can follow from this exercise, such as, Are there feelings they don't let themselves feel or that they hide? How do they usually behave when scared, angry, sad? Does that behavior tend to help solve the problem or does it make things worse? How do they feel when someone else is angry, sad, scared?

You may want to ask the class to agree that they will all use the main feelings when talking about feelings. You can also use the exercise to build agreements or contracts with the children concerning how they will behave when they have certain feelings. For instance, you may have several children who provoke fights when angry or who pout and withdraw when angry or sad. Such children can be taught to think about what they want and to ask for that.

HOW TO TEACH PEOPLE TO LISTEN
TO THEIR THOUGHTS

ACTIVITY 4—LISTENING TO YOUR THOUGHTS

Rationale: Another important aspect of intrapersonal communication is your thoughts. You may tend to carry on a fairly constant monologue or dialogue in your mind. Much of your thinking involves the processing of information, as when you are driving and thinking about the red light at the next intersection. However, a great deal of what goes on in your mind consists of self-statements, commentaries on your actions, imagined conversations, or worries about upcoming events. So much of your thinking is automatic that often you probably tend not to really listen to yourself.

As with bodily sensations and feelings, becoming aware of your thoughts can provide useful information about yourself. The way that you think about yourself, your abilities, and how others will respond to you has a great deal to do with how you behave. For instance, if I go for a job interview thinking I'm not really qualified and don't have a chance of getting the job, I will not present myself very favorably and may even act in ways that insure failure.

Are you carrying on an internal dialogue as you read this? What kind of statements do you make about yourself in your thoughts?

We often neglect to realize that our thoughts and feelings and bodily reactions are *ours*. They are not fixed, nor are they determined by anyone besides ourselves in most cases. You can regain a tremendous amount of personal power when you realize that you determine your thoughts, you decide how you feel, you can take action to feel differently, and you can control bodily functions to a great extent.

As DeRopp states, "Self-observation leads to self-knowledge, self-knowledge to self-mastery."[2] Self-mastery leads to a maximization of choices, to increased freedom, and to the ability to go beyond the self.

Step 1: Instruct the children to get into a comfortable position and to close their eyes. Tell them to just let their minds wander and to pay attention to their thoughts. What are they thinking about? Are they remembering something or looking forward to something? Allow them to sit quietly watching and listening to their thoughts for five to ten minutes.

Step 2: Discuss what kinds of things they were thinking. Ask them how often they really pay attention to their thoughts. What can they learn by listening to what they are thinking? Do they sometimes find themselves talking to themselves in their minds? For instance, do they ever talk themselves out of trying something by what they tell themselves about their ability?

To the Teacher: Awareness is largely a matter of practice in paying attention. You can help the children in your classes become more aware of themselves by simply having them practice these exercises.

ACTIVITY 5—DISTINGUISHING BETWEEN FEELINGS AND THOUGHTS

Rationale: Many of us are not clear about the distinction between feelings and thoughts and believe that we are expressing feelings when in fact we are stating what we think. For instance, I often hear people say, "I feel that we should . . ." which is clearly an expression of what they *think*.

---

[2]Robert S. DeRopp, *The Master Game*, (New York: Dell Publishing Co., 1968), p. 137.

15

Feelings are a primary response to your environment, whereas thoughts are a translation or interpretation of your experiences. You can lose much important information about yourself when you confuse the two.

Step 1: To help children clearly distinguish between feelings and thoughts you can establish a rule that "I feel" can be followed only by one of the main feeling words. Once they clearly identify how they feel, they can *think* about what they need or want to do.

Step 2: Discuss with the children what they think feelings are, what thinking is, and what is the difference between the two. Help them arrive at a clear distinction between them. What do they learn from feelings; what kind of information do feelings provide? What kind of information does thinking provide?

BECOMING AWARE OF WANTS AND NEEDS

Feelings and thoughts and bodily sensations are integrally related to wants and needs. The former give you the raw data from which you can figure out the latter. If I am aware of being angry, I can think about what I wanted that I didn't get, and either figure out a way to get it or figure out something else that I want. When I feel scared, I may want some reassurance or I may need to get some information I lack to solve a problem.

It is useful to distinguish between needs and wants and not to confuse the two. Wants are things or conditions that you desire but without which you can survive. Needs are those psychological and biological conditions we require for survival and safety. By confusing wants with needs, you may make things much more important than they in fact are. For example, you may make something that is an issue of comfort into one of safety or survival.

In both intrapersonal and interpersonal communication, awareness of needs and wants is very important. Your intrapersonal equilibrium is upset when you lose touch with your wants and needs, and you may behave in ways that really don't make sense for you. Similarly, if I am not in touch with my wants and needs in my relationships, I greatly reduce my chances of having satisfying ones.

HOW TO TEACH PEOPLE TO IDENTIFY
WANTS AND NEEDS

ACTIVITY 6—IDENTIFYING WANTS AND NEEDS

Rationale: As children, we are not always taught to think about our wants and needs or to ask for them. Much disruptive classroom behavior probably is the result of children wanting or needing something but not really knowing what that is or how to get it.

Step 1: Once a child has identified how he or she feels, ask what he or she wants or needs. With young children, you could ask, "What will make you feel better?" You may want to suggest something if they do not know what they want or need. Example: if a child is scared, you could suggest that perhaps he would feel better if he were held for a few minutes.

Step 2: After children have had practice in identifying their wants or needs, do not accept an "I don't know" answer. Instead, require them to take a few minutes and think about what they want or need.

To the Teacher: Another useful exercise, especially with older children, is to have them identify what they want in the future, what they want to accomplish, or what they want to get out of a particular situation or experience. Once they have identified some specifics, ask them to think about how they can go about achieving them.

2

Here and There:
Now and Then

BECOMING AWARE OF WHAT IS
HAPPENING AROUND YOU

An essential intrapersonal process has to do with what you let in or are aware of besides your internal sensations, how much you let in, and how you perceive what is around you. This process is referred to as external awareness.

All of us are selectively attentive, noticing some things and not others. We differ also in how much we pay attention and on what senses we rely for our perceptions. In order to organize our awareness, most of us also tend to categorize our experiences.

You will probably find that what you let into your awareness relates to your values and interests. For instance, whereas I will notice the people at a party, you might notice the furnishings of the house. Being a psychologist, I am very interested in people and how they behave, whereas you may value a well-furnished house.

How much you notice of what is happening around you has a great deal to do with how aware you are generally and with how much importance you place on being aware. Some people have an external frame of reference and largely base their feelings, thoughts, and behavior on what others think, feel, and do. Such people are likely also to pay particular attention to their external environment, whereas other people are much more interested in the inner realm of thoughts and ideas.

There is increasing evidence that people differ in the sense modalities they use, as well as much evidence that we learn best by using our "favorite" or "best" sense. For instance, some children learn best when they hear information; thus they rely primarily on their auditory sense. Others must see visual representations or read material in order to learn effectively. Recently, Grinder and Bandler (1976) have shown that people have favorite ways of representing their experiences to themselves which is evident in the way that they talk. They have identified three major representational systems: auditory, visual, and kinesthetic. You can iden-. tify what sense modality you rely on and what your favorite representa- tional system is by listening to the words you use. For instance, I am primarily a visual person, remembering things best when I see them and tending to use a lot of visual words, such as "I see what you mean" and "I'm not clear about that."

The sense modality or representational system you rely on most de- termines in part what your external awareness is. As you identify how you tend to perceive things, you may realize that your other perceptual senses are underdeveloped. By focusing attention on using your less developed senses you can greatly increase your awareness of what is going on around you as well as internally.

You are continually subjected to stimuli from your environment. Pause for a moment and get in touch with all the sounds around you, with what is in your visual field, any tastes or smells, how your body feels, how you feel emotionally, and thoughts you may be having. Reflect on how much of these stimuli you were aware of before you paused. Because you cannot concentrate while trying to pay attention to all of them, you tend to block some out and try to organize your perceptions and experiences. A major way is to categorize experience, grouping in your mind what seems com- mon about several different stimuli. To the extent that this process allows you to understand experience, it is useful. However, some people form rigid categories in their minds, and in the process of categorizing, become very judgmental and closed-minded. If you have a limited number of categories into which all your experiences must fit, you will probably not allow yourself new experiences or you will miscategorize them.

As you read this book, into what categories are you putting yourself? Are you putting the material in this book into a preconceived category?

Becoming aware of how other people affect you is another important aspect of awareness, both external and internal. Often the influence others have on you is quite subtle and difficult to understand. Other times, your reactions to people are very obvious, pronounced, and clear.

It is important to tune into how you feel around other people because your feelings of comfort or discomfort, liking or disliking, trust or distrust, all affect you and your behavior. By being aware of your reactions you can increase positive control over yourself. When I am able to realize that I am afraid of someone, I can think about why I am afraid and see if it makes sense to me. I can decide to stop being afraid, to avoid that person, or to talk to him or her about my fear. I may also discover something about myself in that process. However, if I am reacting fearfully to someone without realizing it, I certainly cannot resolve my fear and I may do or say things I really don't mean.

Some of the most subtle influences people have on us concern the exchange of energy. Have you ever felt inexplicably drained and tired after being around someone? Conversely, have you felt energized after being with someone else? Those experiences involve energy fields and energy exchanges. Some people seem to be energizing, whereas others rob us of energy. People also differ in the kind of energy they exude. Whereas one person has a calming effect on me, another may leave me feeling nervous and jumpy.

Your reactions to others have a great deal to do with *your* personalities, *your* conflicts, *your* attitudes and feelings about *yourself*. Often when I feel critical of a friend, I realize I am reacting to something in him or her that I don't like in myself. In the process of becoming aware and questioning your reactions to others, you can gain a great deal of self-understanding and increase the choices you have in your behavior.

ACTIVITY 7—TUNING INTO THE ENVIRONMENT

Rationale: The younger children are, the less likely they are to tune out various environmental stimulation and the more limited their ability to concentrate for long periods of time. However, even very young children develop the ability to ignore noises, sights, smells, and other stimuli extraneous to their focus of concentration. This ability seems to develop somewhat automatically, without conscious awareness.

This activity is designed to help children become aware of how much they tend automatically to tune out. Some children may also learn that they do not tune out enough to allow themselves to concentrate on school activities.

Step 1: Have the children sit quietly in their usual places in the classroom, with their eyes closed for a minute or so.

Step 2: Ask them to hear all the sounds around them, to get in touch with their bodies and how they feel sitting at their desks, to notice any smells in the air, to become aware of any tastes in their mouths, to realize how they are feeling emotionally, and to track the thoughts going through their minds. Next, have them open their eyes, and without moving their heads, become aware of all that they see, including peripheral vision.

Step 3: Mimeograph sheets with *seven* columns labeled Sounds, Physical sensations, Smells, Tastes, Feelings, Thoughts, Sights.

Step 4: Pass out the mimeographed sheets and aks the children to list everything they are aware of in the next five minutes.

Step 5: When they have finished, ask several children to read their lists to the class.

Step 6: Discuss any differences in their lists. Did they realize previously that there was so much going on around and in them? Of how much are they usually aware? How do they tune out so much? What would happen if they always tried to pay attention to everything? Why is it sometimes hard to concentrate on one thing?

To the Teacher: With younger children, the same exercise can be done by asking the group, "What do you hear right now?" "What do you see right now?" etc. They may respond verbally.

Once you have exposed children to this activity you can ask them to become aware of external stimuli whenever you want. When a child or the whole group is having difficulty concentrating, you can help them realize why and to focus their attention.

BECOMING AWARE IN THE HERE AND NOW

Much of your experience can be lost if you do not live primarily in the present. Every second that you are alive, you are experiencing a myriad of complex sensations and stimuli, so much that in fact your brains filter out a great deal in order to allow you to concentrate when you want to. There is evidence that the human mind cannot deal with all the stimuli present at any given time. Much of what we do take in goes "on, spindle" and may be used at a later time.

However, most of us are much less aware moment to moment than we can be, and consequently, miss a great deal of our experience and joy. How many times have you not been totally involved in a situation because you were thinking about what you are going to do tomorrow or next week? How many times have you stopped yourself from enjoying something because you were worried about future consequences? How often do you not hear what somebody says because you're remembering what someone in your past said or did?

The pace of today's society is so rapid that it is hard to slow down or take the time to finish one experience before we begin another. Your ability to integrate experiences is probably considerably slower than your ability to accumulate them. All of us carry around bits and pieces of unfinished business, memories and unintegrated feelings which produce a kind of static or background noise to our experience of the present. What are you thinking or remembering or anticipating as you read this?

You can reduce this background noise by taking the time to become aware in the here and now in any given situation and by tuning into the sensations and stimuli that are around and in you. Much of the learning and behavior problems of children in the classroom are a result of the difficulty they are having being fully present. A child who has just left a very upsetting situation at home is not going to be able to concentrate fully on the reading lesson first thing in the morning. Although it isn't possible to help all the children in your classroom fully integrate all their experiences, you can help them become more aware in the present.

Once you learn how to be fully present, you can regain a great deal of control over yourself and your experience as a human being. If you have important unfinished business or feelings about a person or situation, you can choose either to deal with that or to put it aside. The ability to live in the here and now can greatly enrich your daily experience.

ACTIVITY 8—HERE AND NOW AWARENESS

Rationale: Our moment-to-moment awareness usually includes much of our past experiences and future anticipations, so that we often miss much of what is happening in the present. It is useful to learn how to sort out what you are aware of here and now so that you can be fully present when you choose to be.

Following is a simple exercise borrowed from Gestalt therapy.

Step 1: Ask for two volunteers. Have them come to the front of the class and sit facing each other.

Step 2: Explain that you want them to take turns telling each other what they are aware of right now. Instruct them to include physical feelings; what they see, hear, smell, taste; and any emotions they are feeling. Have them begin each statement with "Right now, I am aware of. . . ."

Step 3: Monitor their statements closely to make sure they report only present awareness.

Step 4: Allow other children a turn.

To the Teacher: Once the children understand how to do this exercise, you can have them write out statements of present awareness. Discussion questions can include the following: "Are you usually really aware in the here and now?" "Why are we not aware in the here and now sometimes?" "What are you usually most aware of—the past, the present, or the future?"

ACTIVITY 9—STAYING IN THE PRESENT

Rationale: The children in your classroom come in every day, bringing with them bits and pieces of what they experienced earlier that morning, what they experienced yesterday or last week, and what they anticipate experiencing today or tomorrow. They may come to school happy, sad, angry, scared, or excited. To immediately begin the day's academic work often does not allow them to finish one thing before they start another. You can help them become more fully present and available for new input with the following activity.

Step 1: Ideally this activity should be carried out in two to four small groups of six to eight children with a teacher or aide in each group; each child should have a chance to talk. Since few schools offer either that teacher-to-student ratio or the flexibility in scheduling, this activity is outlined to allow one teacher to do it with a whole classroom.

Step 2: Discuss how you all came to school today with feelings and thoughts and memories of what you experienced before you got there. Some of you may also be thinking about what is going to happen. Give some examples about yourself and what you brought with you today. Explain how these things can get in your way at school in being able to concentrate on what you're doing at the moment. Discuss how people often go from one thing to another without really finishing what they just experienced.

Step 3: Have the children do the breathing exercise (Activity 1) sitting at their desks to allow them to relax and become centered in themselves for a couple of minutes.

Step 4: Ask them to think about what feelings, thoughts, memories, anticipations, etc. they brought with them today. Ask them what they need to do to finish those experiences so that they can leave them behind or put them aside for the time being.

Step 5: If they can finish an experience in their minds or imagination, ask them to do so. They may need to make a decision about what they are going to do later. If they cannot finish it in their minds, ask them if they can put it aside for the time being. Have them imagine a shelf they can put it on until later. (Allow five to ten minutes for this step.)

Step 6: Tell them to open their eyes and return to the classroom, fully present, when they are ready.

Step 7: Especially at first, you will probably need to discuss how that step was for them. Was anyone not able to finish or put aside an experience?

To the Teacher: This activity is designed for older children of at least junior-high age. Some children will find it difficult and others simply may not be able either to finish old business or to put it aside, particularly if they are very upset. However, many children will be able successfully to complete this activity, and all of them will benefit from becoming more aware of themselves.

Many discussions may follow this exercise, and you can invite the children to participate then or on their own whenever they want.

BECOMING AWARE OF PAST INFLUENCES

To a large extent, you are the product of your past. As discussed earlier, we all carry around many memories and bits of unfinished business from our past which can exert considerable influence on our present experiences and awareness. Often you may find that this influence hinders your ability to be in the here and now and to interact with your environment in healthy, appropriate ways.

Have you had the experience of immediately disliking someone only to realize that he or she reminded you of someone in your past? Have you ever stopped yourself from doing something because once before when you did it, it was unpleasant, only to regret your decision?

You can learn a great deal from your past experiences and can integrate those parts that are valuable. It is important, however, to learn to separate past influences from the present. Then, you can act on your old information, on current information, or a combination of the two.

Most of us have unfinished business with people or experiences. Until you finish that business, you will tend to carry it around and it will affect you in some way. Unfinished business makes it difficult to be fully present. An important intrapersonal skill involves learning how to finish things so that you can leave them with a clear mind, ready to move on.

ACTIVITY 10—FINISHING UNFINISHED BUSINESS

Rationale: For many, many reasons, we all sometimes experience unsatisfactory or incomplete interactions with others. Unless we finish these experiences, if only in our minds, we tend to continue to expend energy on them. We may carry around bad feelings, walk around rehearsing what we wish we had said, or worry about the next time we see the person involved. This reaction interferes with being fully present and makes it difficult, if not impossible, to move on to new experiences.

The following exercise will give children some tools with which to finish experiences.

Step 1: Ask the children to close their eyes, take a few deep breaths, and think about a conversation or interaction or experience they had with someone recently that they didn't like, that was unsatisfactory, or perhaps, that was interrupted.

Step 2: Ask them to get in touch with how they felt and/or feel toward the person. What was unfinished with that person?

Step 3: Ask them to carry on a conversation with that person in their minds. Instruct them to say whatever they want or need to say to that person so that the experience is finished and they end up feeling good and ready to move on. Allow at least five minutes.

Step 4: Before they open their eyes, ask them if there is something they want to say to the person later on in real life or if there is some action they want to take. Give them a minute or two to think about this. Once they have made a decision, ask them to put that aside until they can act on it.

Step 5: Have them open their eyes and discuss how that experience was for them. Did they have difficulty? Were they able to finish their business with the person? etc.

To the Teacher: Another way this exercise can be done is to have someone volunteer to finish his or her business with someone out loud in front of the group. Ask the child to explain what his or her unfinished business is and with whom. Place an empty chair in front of the child and tell him or her to imagine that the person is sitting there. The child may tell the person whatever he or she wants. If appropriate, have the child move to the empty chair and respond to him- or herself as the other person. Have the child continue until he or she reaches a point of resolution.

At times, we all realize that we cannot resolve or completely finish business with someone, perhaps because the other person isn't willing; but we can still finish it in our own minds, for ourselves. This process may entail our saying to ourselves, "I cannot get what I want with this person, and so, I am going to stop trying and move on."

ACTIVITY 11—HAVE I BEEN HERE BEFORE?

Rationale: There is mounting evidence to support the idea that we seek out certain experiences, situations, and people in an attempt to recreate earlier experiences, to reinforce certain beliefs, to learn something, or to finish old business. Nothing occurs outside of the context of our experiences, and a great deal of insight and understanding and increased control over our lives can be gained by identifying its patterns. A friend once commented that when we have a conflict with someone, that person is a teacher for us. There is something to be learned in every experience we have.

This activity consists of a number of questions that can be asked in any situation. When children are in conflict, you can suggest these questions as a way to better understand themselves.

Step 1: Invite children in a conflict to answer the following questions:

1. What is similar about this situation and others I've experienced?
2. When have I ended up feeling this way before?
3. Does this person remind me of someone else?
4. Who else in my life has acted this way or treated me this way?
5. What do I get out of this situation or out of feeling this way? (The "payoff" is not necessarily positive. It may be something like, "I get to decide that nobody likes me and then I don't have to take responsibility for how I act.")
6. What is *my* part in this conflict? How have *I* contributed to it?

Step 2: Once these questions have been considered and answered, ask "What can you learn from this conflict? What can *you* do differently so that it doesn't happen again?"

To the Teacher: In all probability, the older the children with whom you do this activity, the more resistance you will encounter. Many of us have the illusion that in any conflict, one of us is wrong and one of us is right. What is really true in most cases is that both sides have played a part in the conflict. When you admit to your part you gain a lot of power and control because you can do something about yourself and your behavior.

Despite resistance you encounter, invite the children to consider the questions. Numerous discussions can follow this activity, including the whole issue of blame-laying.

3

The Magic Carpet Ride
in the Classroom

BECOMING AWARE OF
FANTASIES AND DREAMS

Roberto Assagioli, author of *Psychosynthesis*, contends that to reach self-understanding we must go beyond just an inventory of the elements of the conscious being, and "an extensive exploration of the vast regions of our unconscious must . . . be undertaken."[1] Fantasies and dreams originate in the unconscious mind and can provide you with much insight into yourself. A common fallacy is that fantasies and dreams are not "real," whereas our waking, conscious state is. Although it is true that fantasies and dreams do not usually actually occur (unless you have developed precognition), they are a very real part of you.

There have been many theories about dreams and their origin. In all likelihood, nobody really knows with certainty why we dream or where dreams originate. The more important question is what you do with your dreams and fantasies and how you integrate those aspects of yourself.

Both dreams and fantasies (which are like waking dreams) offer you the opportunity to communicate with and understand yourself. Many of the

[1]Roberto Assagioli, *Psychosynthesis* (New York: Penquin Books, 1976), p. 21.

experiences you filter out of your conscious mind are nevertheless registered. Much that you do not deal with in your conscious, waking hours you will encounter and deal with in your dreams.

Some people believe that dreams and fantasies are of great psychological importance, and some psychotherapy deals almost exclusively with the analyses of dreams or the use of fantasy. However, it is not necessary to be either a psychologist or in therapy to benefit from your dreams and fantasies and to use them to learn about yourself. I once had a fantasy or image of myself at three years old standing in the rain in the middle of a plain all alone. The feelings that went with the image were sadness and fear. From this image, I learned that I sometimes feel abandoned and forlorn. It also symbolized the lack of loving and nurturing I experienced as a child and let me know that I still needed to resolve that issue.

Fantasy or daydreaming may also be used nonproductively, to avoid being aware in the here and now or to avoid dealing with reality. Most teachers have had children in their classroom who sit and daydream rather than pay attention to what is happening in the classroom. Such children may have important unfinished business or feelings they haven't integrated, or they may simply have developed the habit of living in their daydreams. They may be bored, or perhaps they have found waking or conscious reality too painful and use daydreams to escape. When daydreaming or fantasy is used to escape, it is usually not productive; a person who escapes into fantasy and away from conscious reality does not integrate the two. Fantasy is the most productive when used to help integrate and broaden experiences.

Occasionally, children and even adults do not know how to distinguish fantasy from conscious reality. When you try to live in a world entirely of your own creation, it very seldom works. Many people who try to do that are considered insane.

Another aspect of dreams and fantasy currently being explored is the transpersonal, the spiritual and psychic properties of dreams. There is increasing evidence that most, if not all, people have some latent psychic ability (Ornstein, 1972; Le Shan, 1975; Pearce, 1977). Our spiritualism and psychic ability seem to be a matter of development; or whether we have developed these aspects in ourselves. Because fantasy and dreams are unconscious processes and are therefore not hindered by intellectual defenses and controls, you can greatly increase both your spiritualism and psychic experiences by being open to them.

ACTIVITY 12—INTEGRATING DREAMS

Rationale: Dreams are a part of the human experience that receive very little attention in our culture. We negate a part of ourselves when we negate their importance. Dreams not only reflect our feelings, conflicts, desires, and fears but also are a direct line of communication between our conscious and unconscious minds.

It has been proven that we dream every night, although many people report that they don't dream. It is true that they may not recall their dreams, which is a matter of being open to remembering and a matter of practice.

Especially young children often have nightmares that they do not know how to handle or integrate. A number of enjoyable and instructive techniques can be used to help children understand and integrate their dreams.

Step 1: Pass out drawing paper. If possible have crayons, paints, pastels, and colored pencils available.

Step 2: Instruct children to draw a dream they had recently (last night, if they recall it). If they report that the dream was too long to draw, have them pick one part of it or let them draw several pictures. If they dreamed in color, ask them to try to remember the colors. If they dreamed in black and white, instruct them to draw it that way, or if they want, to use colors.

Step 3: Invite them to share their pictures with each other. Allow them the right to not share.

Step 4: Discussion of possible interpretations may follow if children are willing. Other discussion questions are, "Where do dreams come from?" "Why do we dream?" "How do we understand dreams?"

OTHER DREAM ACTIVITIES

Ask children to carry on a conversation with the central dream figure in their minds or out loud using the empty chair technique described in Activity 10. They may want to ask the dream figure what he or she or it wants from them. Have them ask the dream figure if he or she or it will be their friend, requesting a symbol, tangible or intangible, of its friendship.

Next have the children draw a picture of the gift they received from the dream figure.

A Gestalt technique particularly helpful in integrating nightmares is to tell the dream from the point of view of the main figure. For instance, if I have a dream about a man shooting me, using this technique I would tell the dream, as the man in the first person, present tense. This technique is often successful in stopping recurring nightmares.

To the Teacher: Dreams use the language of symbols, and dream interpretation can be a complex endeavor. However, you do not need to be an expert on dreams or worry about interpretations in the above activities. If you approach dreams from the perspective that everything in the dream is a part of you, a reflection of your feelings, conflicts, experiences, etc., much of their mystery is dispelled.

INTUITIVE AWARENESS

In his book *Psychological Types*, Jung (1923) defined two perceptual processes: sensing and intuiting. Sensing involves the use of the five senses and relies on the presence of tangible objects and observable phenomena. Intuiting is perception by way of the unconscious. This definition dispels the notion that intuition is some sort of magical phenomenon and recognizes that it is a valuable, real, and useful means by which learning and knowing occurs.

Most of you have probably had the experience of knowing something you can't really explain how you knew, or of having a hunch or "gut feeling" about something, only to find out later that you were right. This is intuition.

When your intuition remains unused, you are incomplete in your development. Intuition provides you with a way of knowing, an approach to reality, and a means of understanding yourself and others that is unique. Unlike analytical thinking processes, intuition does not work from part to whole, but is a synthesizing, integrating function which apprehends the totality. Intuition is immediate and direct perception, unlike thinking, which is progressive.

By developing and using your intuition, you can expand your awareness and self-understanding. Often when I am unable to decide a course of action based on the facts, my intuition will provide an idea or understanding that is accurate and right.

Intuition takes the information and data available of which you may or may not be consciously aware, and integrates that into a functional whole. Assagioli (1976) emphasized the importance of intuitive processes: "Only intuition gives true psychological understanding both of ourselves and of others."[2]

ACTIVITY 13—DEVELOPING INTUITION

Rationale: All of us have intuitive ability, although in many people, it has either not been developed or been repressed. Intuition is usually accurate, and if you trust it, you will discover that you are right in most cases.

Young children are intuitive naturally, but because they are not as verbal as adults, they don't often talk about their intuitions. Somewhere along the line, many people stop using their intuitive perception as they grow up, probably because of the cultural value placed on reason and rationality and empirical evidence. Intuition is valuable because it does not rely only on what can be observed and can supply information you cannot otherwise obtain.

Step 1: Ask the children to consider, with their eyes closed, a question about someone that they would like to answer. This may be a question about another person or about themselves.

Step 2: Instruct them only to think about the question, not about the answer. Suggest that they use intuition to answer the question. Explain that their intuitive answer may not immediately make sense to them, but to let it occur anyway. Their intuition may supply an image or a song or piece of music or a color or sets of colors or a variety of other possibilities.

Step 3: Invite the children to consider the answer their intuition provided. If it doesn't make sense right now, ask them to remember it and see if sometime later it makes more sense. If the level of trust in the group is high, you may want to invite them to share their experiences.

[2]*Ibid.*, p. 220.

Step 4: Undoubtedly, some of them will not be able to produce an answer. Their difficulty could be caused by many things. They may not have been able to suspend their rational thinking processes; they may not have developed a receptivity to intuitive processes; they may simply not be willing or ready to answer the question they asked.

To the Teacher: The development of active and accurate intuition often requires practice in suspending the rational, reasoning thinking process and in opening the mind to unconscious perception. Our culture teaches men to think rather than to feel or intuit, but women are given a lot of permission to be intuitive and to be in touch with feelings. Therefore, boys and men may experience more difficulty in releasing their intuition.

4

The Day
You Talked to Yourself
and Someone Answered

INTRAPERSONAL PROBLEM SOLVING

At times, you have problems or decisions to make that you must work out for yourself. The process of making decisions is an important one which should not be left to impulse or circumstances. Solving problems effectively for yourself requires a degree of self-knowledge and skill in reviewing that self-understanding.

In order to make "right" decisions for yourself you must be able to identify the problem or conflict and to be aware of your thoughts and feelings. You must also be able to identify the options or alternatives available to you. Often, people back themselves into a corner or scare themselves into inaction because they do not see the alternatives inherent in a situation or do not know how to create other choices for themselves.

There are many ways in which to arrive at decisions and solve problems for ourselves. Some of these will be discussed in the next chapter. It is important to find a process of intrapersonal problem solving with which you are comfortable and which works for you.

ACTIVITY 14—PROBLEM SOLVING

Rationale: The greatest gifts we can give children are the tools by which they can solve problems. Western education tends to focus on teaching content, the what, rather than the process, the how. Consequently, many adults do not know how to reach adequate decisions, how to go about solving conflicts or problems.

The following method of approaching intrapersonal problem solving is but one possible method. For the purpose of illustration, an example is provided.

Step 1: Define the problem or conflict.

Example: I have a homework assignment due tomorrow but I want to go swimming.

Step 2: Analyze the conflict or problem.

Example: The homework will probably take me two hours. Swimming will take one and one-half hours. I also need to do my chores, eat dinner, take a shower. I have five hours until bedtime.

Step 3: Look at alternatives and their consequences.

Example: (a) I could just do the homework and not go swimming. Then, I'd have plenty of time and I wouldn't get an F, but I'd be angry and disappointed that I didn't swim. (b) I could just go swimming. I'd have fun, but I'd get an F tomorrow and my teacher would probably be angry. (c) I could do both, but I'd really have to rush and I might not do the homework well. (d) I could do the homework tonight and go swimming tomorrow.

Step 4: Weigh the consequences and pros and cons of each alternative and make a decision.

Example: I think my fourth alternative is probably the best because I can't afford to get an F in this class and I don't really like the idea of rushing to do everything tonight. I can go swimming tomorrow for a couple of hours without any conflicts.

Step 5: Take action on decision.

To the Teacher: In teaching children to solve problems, it is important to make sure that they identify as many alternatives as possible. There is sometimes a tendency to identify only two, either/or alternatives. In any situation there are usually at least three choices, and the process of learning to identify them is important and valuable.

Likewise, it is important to learn to consider the consequences of each choice and to decide whether they outweigh the benefits. Part of this process is a willingness to accept the consequences, to realize that an integral part of responsible behavior is accepting the results of that behavior.

SELF-SURVEY ON INTRAPERSONAL PROCESSES

Now that you have worked on developing your intrapersonal communication skills, the following self-survey might help you check your progress. It can serve as support for your progress and can help you to determine whether you need more work in the area of intrapersonal communication.

This instrument can be used prior to starting work on this section or as a follow-up. Like any self-survey instrument, it is only as useful as your willingness to be honest with yourself.

Directions: Place a check mark in the column that best represents your perception of yourself. Please answer every item.

	Never	Sometimes	Usually	Always
1. I am aware of tensing certain muscles in my body as I do it.				
2. I feel my emotions as they occur				
3. I feel controlled by the internal messages I have.				
4. I try to control my feelings as much as possible.				
5. There is no discrepancy between how I feel and how I behave.				

	Never	Sometimes	Usually	Always
6. I believe that most of my thoughts are unimportant.				
7. Most of what I say to myself is negative.				
8. I am in touch with what I want.				
9. I confuse my wants with needs.				
10. When I don't get what I want, I stay angry.				
11. I am able to sort out past experiences and influences from current situations.				
12. I find myself dwelling on past events or worrying about the future.				
13. I have difficulty dealing with a new experience that doesn't fit the categories I use.				
14. I am aware of how I feel about people and how they affect me.				
15. My past experiences determine how I respond to people and situations.				
16. I am aware of the unfinished business that I have.				
17. I consider my dreams and fantasies to be real and important aspects of my experience.				
18. Daydreams and fantasies are an escape for me.				
19. I use fantasy and dreams to better understand myself.				
20. I do not avoid negative or painful feelings.				

_____ + _____ + _____ + _____ = _____
Total
Score

SCORING PROCEDURES

Each item is weighted 1, 2, 3, or 4. Certain items are keyed with the "Always" column, weighted at 4, and others are keyed with the "Never" column, weighted at 4. The following key shows how to score each item:

Items scored 1, 2, 3, 4 (Never = 1 and Always = 4) include numbers 1, 2, 5, 8, 11, 14, 16, 17, 19, 20.

Items scored 4, 3, 2, 1 (Never = 4 and Always = 1) include numbers 3, 4, 6, 7, 9, 10, 12, 13, 15, 18.

Write the appropriate number in the column where you placed a check mark. Add all the numbers in each column and add each column total to get a total score. Place your score on the continuum below and look at the relevant interpretation.

20	50	80

20–29 rectal-cranial inversion
30–39 restricted intrapersonal awareness
40–49 awareness limited to the obvious
50–59 good beginnings, growing awareness
60–69 high level of intrapersonal awareness
70+   intrapersonal overachiever

COMMON ERRORS IN INTRAPERSONAL COMMUNICATION

1. Believing your body and mind are separate, that there is no connection between bodily tensions and symptoms and our feelings and thoughts.
2. Acting as if others have control over how you feel or what you think.
3. Not trusting your feelings, your intuitions, your hunches.
4. Believing that it is selfish or egocentric to focus attention on yourself, to really get to know yourself.
5. Believing that your past experiences have nothing to do with you now.

6. Acting on the basis of "should's" and "have to's" instead of on what you want and choose to do.

7. Programming yourself with negative self-statements.

8. Believing that your dreams and fantasies are not related to what is happening to you in your waking life.

9. Not allowing yourself to feel your emotions or believing that certain feelings are not O.K.

10. Living in the past or future and not being present in the here and now.

11. Confusing observation with interpretation.

12. Thinking you are present in the here and now when you're feeling or thinking on the basis of the past or future.

13. Being unable to resolve seeming opposites in yourself.

14. Confusing talk about something with action.

5

How to Integrate Intrapersonal Communication Skills into the Regular Curriculum

TEACHING LANGUAGE ARTS IN THE PRIMARY GRADES BY USING AWARENESS IN THE HERE AND NOW

Generally young children are very here-and-now oriented. You can increase their interest in learning to read, write, and spell by using their immediate environment in the content of the lessons.

Purpose: To teach reading, writing, and spelling to third graders by using awareness of the here and now.

Procedure: Ask the children to look around the classroom and find something that they really like, are interested in, or about which they would like to learn more. Allow them either to bring the object(s) to their desks or to move their chairs so that the object is right in front of them.

On the blackboard make the following list:

> Right now I see . . .
> Right now I feel or touch . . .
> Right now I hear . . .
> Right now I taste . . .
> Right now I smell . . .

Instruct them to examine carefully the object they have chosen, and as they do, to write on their papers what they see, feel, hear, and taste, beginning each sentence as you have listed on the board. Encourage them to pay attention to everything they can—the color, shape, size, texture, weight, and length of the object.

Circulate around the room as the children are working and help them identify as many aspects of their objects as possible. As they become aware of details, they will probably think of words that they don't know how to spell. Individualized or group spelling lists can be generated and used in future spelling lessons.

When they have completed their lists, ask them what they noticed about their objects that they weren't aware of before. For practice in reading, ask them to read their papers to the rest of the class.

To the Teacher: This kind of activity can be repeated or varied. You may want the entire class to focus on and write about one object; you can have the children close their eyes and verbally describe what they feel, hear, smell, or taste as they hold an object in their hands. You can write their responses on the board and later have the class read them out loud, using this exercise to generate spelling words.

TEACHING SOCIAL STUDIES
IN THE INTERMEDIATE GRADES BY USING
AWARENESS OF FEELINGS AND THOUGHTS

As children learn about different places and cultures in social studies, they often form opinions based upon their reactions to what they have learned. They are seldom consciously aware of the formation of these reactions and opinions because most classes focus only on the facts and content of the lessons. By helping children to become aware of their personal reactions to the facts, you can not only increase their retention but also help them identify how they feel and what they think about what they are learning. They may also discover that their opinions are based on assumptions or biases or that they are overgeneralizing from some past experience or something they may have heard.

Purpose: To show a film on Africa, using awareness of feelings and thoughts as the focus of discussion.

Procedure: Before showing the film, explain that you want to discuss the children's feelings and thoughts about the film when it is over. If your class has not done Activities 3, 4, or 5, or discussed the difference between feelings and thoughts, take a few minutes to define that difference (see Chapter 1). Then show the film.

After they have seen the film, first ask how they felt as they saw it. How do they feel about Africa? About the people who live there? About blacks? You may want to ask how they felt about specific situations depicted in the film. Be sure that they are distinguishing between how they feel and what they think.

Next, ask what they think about Africa, the people who live there, how those people live, etc. They probably will express some opinions or biases or prejudices which you may want to discuss further.

To the Teacher: This procedure can be repeated with almost any content presented to your class. Generally, learning becomes of more value and interest when children have a personal connection with it.

TEACHING INDUSTRIAL ARTS
IN JUNIOR HIGH SCHOOL BY USING
INTRAPERSONAL PROBLEM-SOLVING STRATEGIES

Many children have not learned to think effectively or been given the tools to solve problems. Such children will become dependent on someone else to think and solve their problems for them. If you respond by always supplying the answers, you reinforce and help maintain their dependency.

One of the drawbacks of interacting with children in this manner is that they do not learn to take care of themselves and are robbed of the joy and pride they could experience in their creations and successes. Industrial arts offers an excellent opportunity to foster independent thinking and problem solving.

Purpose: To foster effective, independent thinking and intrapersonal problem-solving skills in industrial-arts classes.

Procedure: Conduct your class as usual, teaching the skills necessary to adequately complete a project. When you are ready for the class to begin their projects, first have them go through the intrapersonal problem-solving strategy outlined in Activity 14, Chapter 4, either in writing or verbally.

To the Teacher: Your role is to facilitate this process and to act as a consultant by helping the students define alternatives and solutions. Consultants ask more questions than they supply answers. Design your questions to encourage children to think and to arrive at their own answers, e.g., "Will that work?" or "What else could you do?"

TEACHING PSYCHOLOGY IN HIGH SCHOOL
BY USING PAST AWARENESS

One of the most effective ways to teach psychology is experientially in which students learn about themselves and the people around them. This kind of approach helps students internalize and integrate what they learn by translating fact and theory into experience.

The most effective psychologists, therapists, or counselors are usually those who know and understand themselves. Many college psychology and counseling programs require students to go through their own therapy or to participate in a variety of experiential workshops.

Purpose: To teach the psychological impact of past experiences on people by having students examine some of their own past experiences.

Procedure: Have students divide into groups of five or six. Ask them to choose at least one person with whom they have had some conflict or with whom they are uncomfortable. Have one person begin by stating with whom he or she has had a conflict and what that conflict is. Have him or her consider and discuss the questions outlined in Activity 11, Chapter 2. Other group members may ask additional questions. They are not to voice their own opinions or conflicts with the person being discussed, however. All statements should be directed to a person, not made *about* a person (avoid third-person pronouns).

Continue until every person in the small groups has had an opportunity to discuss his or her conflict. Start a discussion with all students about this experience. What did they learn? Did they discover some connection between their previous and current experiences? How much do they think people are dominated by past experiences? Is it possible to become liberated from the influences of the past? How?

To the Teacher: One of the values of this exercise is the exposure of students to others' experiences. Often, in a group they will learn more about themselves than they would from self-analysis. This exercise also invites students to be self-disclosing and to learn to give and receive feedback.

This exercise is not designed to be a confrontation; it is intended more as self-confrontation and self-awareness.

II

INTERPERSONAL COMMUNICATION SKILLS

ESSENTIAL INTERPERSONAL COMMUNICATION PROCESS

The importance of interpersonal skills—the ability to meet interpersonal needs and to form and maintain quality relationships—is becoming apparent as we witness the rising increase in divorce, child abuse, violent crime, alcoholism, mental illness, the confusion and disenchantment of young people, and the increasing number of people seeking psychotherapy. Continued technological advances are changing the meaning of work, and we are confronted with more and more leisure time. A diploma or bachelor's degree, or even a master's degree or doctorate, are no longer any guarantee that one will be employed in the field of one's choice. Few people enjoy the ongoing support and satisfaction of interpersonal needs once provided by a stable family system. Instead, most people's families are spread all over the country or world; and even if they live in close proximity to each other, many are not close emotionally.

All these factors and many others too numerous to list are creating stresses on the individual that few can or would choose to tackle by themselves. *People need people.* Most of us would be desperately unhappy without close, significant, meaningful relationships. Thus, the need to acquire interpersonal communication skills is more acute than ever.

In an article in the *Journal of Humanistic Psychology*, Peterman states,

> Consistently meeting basic interpersonal needs over time probably requires formation and maintenance of a number of relationships of very high quality, and that is likely to occur only to the extent that certain values and skills exist which are rather different from the ones currently supported and developed by our culture. Obviously, we are not now doing what is necessary to prepare the growing person to meet the developmental task of successfully forming such a cluster of relationships. . . . For individuals to meet their interpersonal needs, two very distinct cultural shifts must occur . . . we shall have to build training programs in interpersonal skills into our educational system, so that people generally become more competent at initiating and maintaining growth-enhancing relationships. . . .[1]

We have identified the following essential interpersonal processes which are discussed in this section:

1. attending to verbal and nonverbal communication
2. establishing ground rules for basic communication
3. paraphrasing
4. listening and giving relevant responses
5. being aware of nonverbal communication
6. expressing feelings effectively
7. dealing with feelings in others
8. developing effective thinking and problem-solving skills
9. confronting discounting and passivity
10. developing cooperation
11. using contracting
12. developing self-disclosure
13. meeting wants and needs effectively
14. clarifying values

---

[1]Dan J. Peterman, "Toward Interpersonal Fulfillment in an Eupsychian Culture," *The Journal of Humanistic Psychology*, 12, No. 1 (Spring 1972), 72–85.

6

Stop,
Look, and Listen

**LEARNING HOW TO PAY ATTENTION TO VERBAL
AND NONVERBAL COMMUNICATION**

As human beings, we spend a tremendous amount of time trying to communicate with each other. As teachers, counselors, or parents, the major part of your job and your role is that of a communicator. How often are you effective in getting across the message you intend? How often do you misunderstand what others are trying to tell you?

Effective communication exists only when two conditions are met. First, the message the sender is giving must accurately reflect his or her intentions. Then, the receiver must interpret the message in the same way the sender intended it.

Consider how complex a process that really is. Have you had the experience of trying to communicate something only to discover that the message you actually conveyed was different than you intended? Perhaps your tone of voice, your stance, facial expressions, or gestures communicated one thing while your voice said another. You may have learned something about yourself in such a process. You have probably also been misinterpreted by someone even though your communication was clear, your verbal and nonverbal communication were congruent, and you said exactly what you intended. However, something happened in the other person's perceptual process to cause misunderstanding. Perhaps he or she only half listened or was upset already and read something into what you said, or perhaps the person defined some of your words differently than you do.

At best, communication is a difficult and complex process requiring much skill and training. Yet, we tend to assume that all we have to do is speak and we will be understood, and that if we hear what someone says in response, we have communicated. It is true we have communicated something. *What* we have communicated is another question.

Verbal communication—the exchange of words—is difficult enough. Add to that the whole realm of nonverbal communication, body language and behavior, and the task of communicating effectively can become overwhelming. What does it mean when someone says caring words with no facial expression? How do you interpret a denial of anger stated in an angry tone of voice? What does it mean when I say one thing and do something else? What I am really saying if, as I agree with you, I am shaking my head "no"? How do we form first impressions? What do we pick up from how people look, walk, carry themselves, and gesture, movements from which we unconsciously form judgments?

Unless we have gone through some special training, most of us are not aware of our own or others' verbal and nonverbal communication. Effective communication is not only necessary for the transfer of information, so important to the learning process, but also largely determines the kinds of relationships we have and how successful, close, trusting, and satisfying they are.

You can greatly improve communication in your classroom, as well as equip children with very necessary interpersonal skills, by helping them learn to pay attention to verbal and nonverbal communication. Following are some basic guidelines, skills, and exercises to increase awareness of communication.

BASIC GUIDELINES FOR COMMUNICATION

1. Say "I" when you are expressing something that you think or feel or have done instead of using words like "you," "they," "people," etc.

Thus you acknowledge that what you are saying is about you, and thereby let people get to know you.

2. Avoid asking questions unless you really need information or need to know something. Often questions are an indirect way of making statements and a way to shift responsibility onto someone else. For example, "Don't you think that . . . ?" is a sneaky way of making a statement without taking responsibility for it.

3. Avoid discounting, which is acting as if what *you* think or feel is more important than what the other person thinks and feels, or denigrating yourself and acting as if the other person is more important than you. Some examples of discounting are
    a. interrupting (discounting the person talking)
    b. not speaking because you think you'll sound stupid (self-discounting)
    c. not taking the other person's desires into account, e.g., deciding what you will do on a date (discounting the other person)
    d. saying things that put yourself down (self-discounting)

The opposite of discounting is accounting—taking you, your feelings, thoughts, and desires, into account along with the other person.

4. Don't rescue, which is doing for someone what he or she can do for him- or herself. This is a discount of the other person because you are acting as if he or she can't take care of himself or herself.

5. Avoid interpreting. An interpretation is when you tell someone what motivates them, why they feel or think or act the way they do, for example, "You are an angry person." The main reason this is not a very good way to communicate is that the other person will probably feel defensive.

It is more effective and straightforward to tell the person how *you* feel or what *you* think; make your statement from an "I" position ("I think . . .") or describe what it is that makes you think as you do, for example:
    a. You're a defensive person. [interpretation] I notice that you argue and disagree with most of the things I say, and it's hard for me to talk to you. [describing what you feel and think]

6. There is a difference between feelings and thoughts, although we often confuse the two in language. For instance, "I feel that you are wrong about that" is actually a thought, not a feeling. Only use "I feel . . ." when expressing feelings (anger, sadness, fear, happiness, fatigue, etc.).

51

7. Avoid using exaggerations or exaggerated words such as "always," "never," "incredible," "the most . . . in the world," etc. This is often a way of justifying your ineffectiveness, avoiding a problem, or avoiding responsibility for your behavior; for example, "I was so angry, I couldn't help myself." The fact is that you could help yourself.

8. Avoid qualifying statements or phrases, such as "perhaps," "maybe," "I guess," unless you *really* are unsure. Such words are often a way of avoiding responsibility for what you say. Likewise, the word "try" is often used as a way of really saying, "I won't do it." Trying is very different from *doing*.

9. Avoid such statements as "I can't" and "I have to" unless that is really the case. It is rare that we actually are unable or incapable of doing something and rarely true that we "have to" do anything, unless someone is physically forcing us. What is true is that we choose to act the way we do in most cases, often because if we did not we would suffer unpleasant consequences.

10. Confront other people's misstatements. Confrontation is a sign of caring. When you ignore or go along with someone's game-playing, discounting, etc., you are actually hurting that person and acting as if you don't care. You can confront in a caring way without attacking the person or his or her behavior.

11. Take responsibility for how you feel, think, and behave. Don't say, "You made me angry," because that makes your feelings someone else's responsibility. Instead say, "I am angry because . . ." (and state your reasons). Avoid saying "makes me feel."

ACTIVITY 15—GROUND RULES FOR INTERPERSONAL COMMUNICATION

These guidelines present interesting material for group discussion and a basis upon which to build other skills in communication. You can also ask that everyone in the group agree to use these guidelines and to confront each other and themselves when they are violated.

Step 1: Hand out lists of the guidelines to each student. Read aloud, or have students read aloud, each of the guidelines one by one.

Step 2: Ask for discussion on each. Do they agree or disagree? Why? Have they heard other people violate these guidelines? What happens? How do they feel? Do they ever violate these guidelines? What examples of discounting, or rescuing, or interpreting can they think of?

Step 3: Ask if anyone can think of other guidelines for communication that are important. Add them to the list if they are appropriate.

Step 4: Ask that everyone agree to communicate according to these guidelines when in the group. To avoid negative interchanges, also agree upon how violations of the guidelines will be confronted. For instance, when someone says "you" instead of "I," a good confrontation might be, "Whom are you talking about?"

To the Teacher: In Chapter 8, confrontation skills are discussed. To avoid hurt feelings, defensiveness, and fights, we suggest you familiarize yourself and your class with ways to confront effectively and with caring.

The children should also be cautioned not to impose what they have learned on other people or to suddenly start confronting people outside the group. They may want to take the guidelines home and show them to their families or friends. Then, they could ask if these other people are willing to use them.

ACTIVITY 16—PARAPHRASING

Rationale: To reduce the miscommunication that occurs when the receiver misinterprets the sender's message, paraphrasing is a useful skill. It also has a feedback effect to the sender and may point out to him or her that the message was unclear.

Paraphrasing is stating in your own words what you think somebody said. A paraphrase can be prefaced with, "Are you saying . . ." "Do you mean . . ." "What I think you said is. . . ." Be careful to avoid interpretations, assignment of meaning, or motivation.

Step 1: Ask for two volunteers to carry on a conversation about a topic in front of the class. Topics might be their opinion of the president of the United States, what they think about prejudice, etc.

Step 2: Instruct the two volunteers in paraphrasing and give several examples.

Step 3: After one of them makes a statement, the other is to paraphrase it. After the paraphrase, the person paraphrasing should check to see if the paraphrase was accurate by saying, "Is that right?" If the communication is clear, they may continue their discussion, paraphrasing after each statement.

Step 4: Allow other students to volunteer.

To the Teacher: Until the group as a whole has had some practice and has learned the difference between paraphrasing and interpreting, you will have to monitor this exercise. Some children may have a lot of difficulty learning how to paraphrase. They also have a tendency to try to repeat exactly what the person said. Encourage them to paraphrase in *their own words.*

Another method is to have students pair up with a partner, so that the whole group is doing the exercise simultaneously. This variation could follow the activity as outlined once the group understands what paraphrasing is.

ACTIVITY 17—NOT LISTENING AND GIVING IRRELEVANT RESPONSES

Rationale: Much miscommunication involves not really listening and/or not making relevant responses to what has been said. "Chaining" occurs when person B responds to person A's statement with one indirectly related to it. This kind of response fouls communication and makes it impossible for two people to actually connect or resolve anything.

The following exercise is a way of teaching the difference between listening and not listening and making relevant or irrelevant responses.

Step 1: Ask for a group of four to six volunteers to come up in front of the group and carry on a conversation. Give them an interesting topic to discuss.

Step 2: Tell them that they are to respond to each other with statements that are *not* directly related to what each of them says, and give them some examples. (One person says, "People who are prejudiced and put blacks down are really just afraid of them," and another person replies, "I had a really good black friend once.")

Step 3: Have them continue their conversation for about five minutes.

Step 4: Ask them how they felt getting such responses? Have they ever had such conversations? What happens to communication in these kinds of conversations? Where did the conversation begin and where did it end? Were the statements even on the same subject?

Step 5: Let others volunteer for the same exercise if there is time.

Step 6: Have the same group(s) have another conversation. This time they are to paraphrase what each other says. After paraphrasing, they may make a statement *related* to the statement they just paraphrased, expressing their opinions, thoughts, or feelings.

Step 7: Discuss how they felt in this conversation. What was different about the two conversations? Did they feel different? In which conversation was the communication more clear, complete, or effective?

To the Teacher: A variation of this exercise is to break into small groups so everyone is involved; then a large group discussion can follow. We suggest you first have a small group demonstrate the exercise.

You can build on this exercise by asking if everyone is willing to monitor themselves in daily interchanges and to be sure they are listening and responding to each other.

NONVERBAL COMMUNICATION

Probably as much as 60 percent of the social meaning of communication is conveyed by nonverbal messages. Thus, awareness of nonverbal communication is of paramount importance in becoming an effective communicator.

The primary way feelings are communicated is nonverbally. In particular, facial and vocal cues communicate how we feel about people. For instance, the presence or absence of eye contact between people as they talk is usually a good indicator of how close and trusting they are. Smiling, frowning, the way that we look at each other, and the tone of voice we use convey our feelings about someone immediately.

A major problem with nonverbal communication is that it tends to be ambiguous. Any given nonverbal expression may reflect a number of feelings. Fear may be nonverbally expressed by physical restlessness and agitation or by immobility. Close physical proximity may mean a person wants to be close, but it may also signal aggression or provocation.

The ambiguity of nonverbal communication compounds the task of interpreting communication accurately. It also makes the sender's job more difficult if he or she is attempting to communicate effectively and clearly. Has a friend or co-worker ever assumed that you were angry or upset because of the way you walked into the room, when in fact you were neither?

Additional problems occur when our nonverbal communication contradicts our verbal interaction. Which is the receiver supposed to accept as the sender's intended meaning? How do we reconcile the lack of congruence between verbal and nonverbal messages?

To be truly effective in your communication, you must be skilled in both verbal and nonverbal modes and make both messages consistent with each other. As a receiver, you must be alert to both modes of communication and be aware of the congruence or incongruence in the verbal and nonverbal messages you receive.

Following are some activities designed to increase awareness of nonverbal communication.

ACTIVITY 18—EYE CONTACT

Rationale: Eye contact is one of the most intense forms of communication and also one of the most ambiguous. In one situation, it is a way to become intimate and close, to communicate openness and trust between two people. In another situation, it is a challenge, an act of aggression. Avoidance of eye contact may indicate shyness or embarassment or a desire to avoid confrontation or communication. In another situation, it may indicate the presence of intense feelings the person does not wish to show others. In yet another situation, it may mean someone is deep in thought or daydreaming.

In the absence of conflict or aggressive feelings, prolonged eye contact is a way to get close, to really experience another person in a very open way, especially if there is no talking. Often we know more about people in a few seconds of looking in their eyes than we can in hours of talking.

Step 1: Have the children get into pairs, either by assignment or by choice.

Step 2: Have them sit cross-legged on the floor, facing each other.

Step 3: Tell them that they are to spend a few minutes looking into each other's eyes without talking. (Start with about two minutes, especially with younger children. Don't exceed about five minutes.) Tell them that, as much as they are able, they are to look directly at each other without looking away. Discourage laughter.

Step 4: Ask them to talk about how they felt. Was it difficult? Did they want to look away or move or talk? Discuss what happens when people really look at each other. Do they feel close, vulnerable, scared, etc.? Under other circumstances, what kinds of feelings can eye contact bring up? Do they usually look directly at people when they talk to them? Do they sometimes avoid eye contact? Why? When?

To the Teacher: This can be an intense experience and can also be rather frightening at times. Judge how long to have them maintain eye contact by their maturity, age, ability to concentrate, and the closeness of the group. You may want to start out for only one minute.

ACTIVITY 19—NONVERBAL PLAYS

Rationale: To help children become aware of the wide range of nonverbal communication.

Step 1: Find a short play, write one, or have the children write one. With younger children you may want to use a situation they are to act out.

Step 2: Depending upon time, you may want to let the children presenting the play rehearse it first. Otherwise, let them read the play and decide how they are going to act out their parts. With younger children, you may want to read each line of the play or event in the situation and then have it acted out.

Step 3: The children may not talk or make noises as they do this exercise.

Step 4: After the performance, ask the audience to describe what they think the play or situation was about. Discussion of the wide range of nonverbal communication we all use can follow.

To the Teacher: Variations of this activity could include the popular game of charades or mime.

ACTIVITY 20—WINDOWS TO THE SOUL

Rationale: Our eyes and what we reflect in them are one of the most expressive aspects of our communication. With rare exceptions, our eyes will tell how we are feeling. This activity is designed to help people become aware of the expressive nature of eyes and also to learn more about how they use their own eyes.

Step 1: Divide the group into small groups of three or four. Explain that they are going to express feelings with their eyes and may use only their eyes. They may not talk, make noise, move, or use gestures.

Step 2: Ask the members of each group to look at each other and notice each others' eyes as they are now sitting.

Step 3: Now ask them to feel scared and to show that fear in their eyes, looking at the others in their group as they do so. Give them a minute to do this step.

Step 4: Ask them to show anger in their eyes.

Step 5: Then ask them to show sadness.

Step 6: Ask them to show happiness.

Step 7: Discuss how they experienced this exercise. Was it hard to use only their eyes? Could they tell how others were feeling just by their eyes? Have they noticed how people's eyes reflect what they are feeling?

To the Teacher: Some children may find this activity difficult, and you may see them using facial expressions. Encourage them to use only their eyes. Children may also find this exercise embarrassing, and you may need to discourage laughter.

EXPRESSING FEELINGS EFFECTIVELY

Feelings are a natural form of response to your environment and to other people. As discussed in Section I, feelings are a source of self-information and a form of energy which can be used to solve problems. There are no "bad" feelings. Anger, fear, and sadness are normal, healthy responses to certain situations or events.

What we do with our feelings can be healthy and productive or unhealthy and destructive. To express anger violently, physically or verbally, is destructive and creates additional problems. On the other hand, completely to deny or repress anger is equally nonproductive.

A healthy, productive, and effective way to express feelings to another person in a way that promotes solving problems is to state how you are feeling, the reasons for your feeling, and what you want from that person:

> I feel [angry, sad, scared, etc.] because [reason]. What I want from you is [change in behavior, etc.].
> Will you do that?

In order to use feelings as a source of energy, it is very important to identify what it is that you want changed or how things can be changed to eliminate or ameliorate the problem. Once you have stated what you want from other people, it is also important to see if they are willing to comply with your request. If they are unwilling, you can explore other alternatives. You may be able to reach a compromise, or you may realize you must change something, such as your expectations or behavior.

When you are very angry or scared or sad you may not be immediately able or willing to express your feelings in this manner. You may first need to release, experience, and feel those emotions. As with communicating feelings, there are healthy and unhealthy ways of releasing them. Punching a hole in a wall may release some energy, but it damages property and is likely to hurt. A loud scream, punches on pillows or a punching bag, and physical exercise are nondestructive ways of releasing anger. When very sad, you may need to cry for awhile.

Once you have released feelings, communicated how you're feeling, and asked for what you want, it is appropriate to let go of those feelings and be done with them. Many people hang onto feelings, using them as a weapon either against others or themselves. Sometimes you will encounter a problem you can't solve, and you may need the resolve to put your energy elsewhere.

Following is a behavioral progression for dealing with feelings in a healthy manner:

1. Person becomes aware of an unmet need or want, which leads to
2. feelings (sadness, fear, anger), which if the person has permission to feel, will lead to
3. thoughts about the need or want and related needs and wants and
4. how these are connected to significant persons in the environment and to this specific situation, which leads to
5. the person generating options for meeting the need or want, which leads to
6. a decision to act on one of the options, which
7. turns the feelings of fear, sadness, or anger into excitement; if the option leads to success, then the feelings will be happy or joyful.

DEALING WITH FEELINGS IN OTHERS

When you perceive feelings in another person, whether expressed verbally or nonverbally, it is important to acknowledge those feelings and/or to verify the accuracy of your perception. You can ask, "Are you angry?" or "You look really sad. Are you?" When someone comes to you and says, "I'm really mad because . . ." it is important to acknowledge that you hear they are angry by saying something like, "I hear that you're really mad. Is there something that you want from me?" or "What do you need to do to get glad?"

Ignoring or denying another's feelings is a discount, and such responses encourage unhealthy ways of dealing with feelings. Responses like "There's nothing to be afraid of" or "You shouldn't be angry" really deny people's right to feel what they feel. They may react to such statements by denying their own feelings or escalating them.

Some of us have learned to be scared of certain feelings, perhaps because of our experiences as children. I used to be very frightened of anger because I thought it meant, automatically, that someone didn't like or love me. My response made it impossible for the other person and me to resolve our problem. Other people may be scared or disgusted by the expression of sad feelings, like crying. Such a response, whether expressed through body language or verbally, may inhibit the other person's expression.

A common misconception is that when someone else is scared or sad or mad, you must do something about it. Thus, some people experience other people's expression of feelings as a demand. You may *choose* to do something, such as to put your arm around someone who is sad, but their feelings are *not* your responsibility.

In a relationship in which you do have some responsibility for the person, such as parent-child or teacher-child, or a relationship in which you have a contract to behave in specific ways, such as therapist-client, you do have responsibility for responding in ways that promote healthy expression and handling of feelings. You are still not responsible for others' feelings or for solving their problems, however.

Following are some suggested responses to the expression of feelings:

Feeling	*Definition*	*Suggestion on What to Say*
1. Anger	A response to not getting a want or need met. May not have permission to express anger and is scared too.	"Wow, you are really angry about something." "Do you want to talk about it?"
2. Fear	Person perceives physical or emotional danger. May not have permission to think and feel at the same time. May be covering anger. Person lacks necessary information to deal with a situation.	"You look afraid of something. Do you want to talk about it with me?" "You can be scared and still think about what you want or need." "The scared feeling is telling you to think of something that would make things better."
3. Sadness	The loss of a person, thing, or relationship (real or fantasy). It is an important part of "giving up" something you are attached to. There may be some anger connected with the loss.	"You are looking sad today. Will you talk to me about it?" "It's O.K. to feel sad about that." "It's O.K. to be mad about losing that, too."
4. Excitement	Anticipation of something good happening. Fear and excitement are closely related. Some children don't have permission to show excitement.	"You are really excited about your birthday party." "It's O.K. to feel good about the plans you have made."
5. Happiness or Joy	Satisfaction in getting what you wanted or needed, or doing something effectively. Some people don't know it's acceptable to be effective and to be happy.	"You look really pleased about the story you wrote." "It's really neat that you took care of yourself by asking for what you wanted."

All feelings are not straightforward or appropriate or healthy responses to situations. If you grew up in a family where anger was not permitted, you may have learned to become scared or to cry when you are really angry. The definitions listed above and also in Section I for the five basic feelings can be helpful in determining whether someone's feelings coincide with what they are experiencing. The person who is confusing feelings, who is unclear about what he or she is feeling, or who lacks permission to feel certain emotions may need to hear that it is all right to have those feelings. Your report of how you would feel in such a situation may also help them become clear about how they are feeling and give them the permission they need.

In dealing with feelings in others, it is also helpful to ask them to be precise and specific about how they feel. Vague words such as "uptight," "upset," "bummed out" or "weird" do not define for the person or you whether they are angry, sad, scared, or some combination thereof. Other feeling words are used as a way to avoid or deny feelings. Words like "frustrated," "annoyed," and "irritated" usually cover anger. Fear may be covered over with words like "nervous," "jumpy," "tense," "uneasy," or "confused." "Lonely," "down," "empty," and "low" may mean "sad." When you hear such words, it is useful to ask the person to clarify how he or she is feeling, which will also help you avoid misinterpretation. You can ask, "What does uneasy mean to you? Are you feeling scared?"

Some of the feeling words we use actually reflect a combination of feelings. For instance, "guilty" is usually a combination of "scared" and "angry." "Disappointed" often means "I am angry and sad." It is useful to ask the person to define what the combination of feelings is so that everyone understands the problem. This clarification also makes it easier for the person to figure out what he or she needs or wants.

Depression is often confused with sadness, when in fact the two are quite distinct. Depression often has some sadness in it, but the function and usually the experience of the two feelings are different. Sadness is related to a loss, and we can use it productively to say "good-bye," to give up the lost person or object or situation. Depression often reflects the internalization of anger, a turning of the anger on oneself instead of outwardly. Depression is also usually a state of withdrawal and inaccesibility to stimulation or to a specific situation. It may be precipitated by a loss, in which case it may be a combination of anger and sadness and withdrawal.

Activity 3 in Section I can be used effectively in the teaching of interpersonal as well as intrapersonal communication.

HOW TO TEACH EFFECTIVE THINKING
AND PROBLEM-SOLVING SKILLS

Many children come to school having already decided not to think effectively and not to solve problems. The way that you relate to them will either reinforce that decision or help them change it. Many of the problems school-age children have in thinking are the result of adaptive patterns, in which they have gotten their parents or other adults to do their thinking and problem solving for them (unhealthy symbiosis). This pattern is a natural occurrence in children before the age of two, but if parents don't begin to transfer the responsibility, children don't learn to think and take care of themselves in appropriate ways. Teaching children to think and solve problems then becomes an important task of yours. This is part of the process of teaching responsibility (response-ability), or the ability to think and respond appropriately in a situation. Being responsible, therefore, means doing or saying what you already know is appropriate to do or say in a situation.

Children use passivity and discounting to avoid thinking for themselves. If you recognize these behaviors, you will be able to confront them effectively and help children to solve problems.

PASSIVE BEHAVIORS AND HOW TO CONFRONT THEM EFFECTIVELY

Behavior	Reasons for the Behavior	What to Say and Do
1. Doing nothing. Frequently may say "I don't know" when faced with a problem. Shy children may do this often. May not answer questions. May engage in long silences before answering simple questions.	Hopes that you will do the thinking. Learned that appearing weak and helpless got someone else to think for them.	"I know you have that information, so why don't you think about it and let me know when you have." "If you need information that you don't have you can ask for it." "Think about what you need from me (or others) and ask for it."
2. Overadaptation. This is often the most difficult to recognize because children do exactly as they are told. They try to	People in this position don't learn reasons for things. Usually have faulty understanding of cause-and-effect relationships. This	"What are your reasons for doing that?" "People have reasons for doing what they do and I expect you to know them." "I expect you

Behavior	Reasons for the Behavior	What to Say and Do
figure out what you want them to do, not what they want to do.	behavior leaves the responsibility to solve the problem with another person. To overadapt is to do what someone else wants you to do or what you *think* they want you to do.	to think about what you want to do and why you want to do it." Need to make sure the person sets his own goals, which take into account (1) what is appropriate for the situation, (2) his or her feelings, and (3) other people's feelings.
3. Agitation. These are nonproductive repetitive behaviors (tapping a pencil, chewing on an eraser, pacing back and forth, talking without saying anything new).	They are attempts to avoid solving a problem. Hope to wait out someone or make him or her uncomfortable enough so he or she solves the problem.	"Stop that and think about what you want." "Instead of doing that, I want you to put energy into solving the problem."
4. Incapacitation or violence. This includes temper tantrums, developing physical symptoms or fainting, having a seizure, etc. Or it could take the form of violence—kicking, hitting, or breaking something or someone.	This is a more desperate attempt to get someone else to take responsibility. Following the discharge of energy is a good time to give these children messages about how to think and solve problems more effectively.	Take whatever steps are necessary to restore order or control. The person is out of control, and at that point taking control is a very direct and appropriate step. Following the blow up: "It is not O.K. for you to solve problems that way." "Think about what you could have done instead to solve problems."

DISCOUNTING

Instead of solving problems, people often suffer about them and engage in discounts about them. They may block their feelings, pretending that there isn't a problem. To do so they may get giddy, depressed, or engage in repetitive behavior. Or they may deny the significance of a problem, saying that they are not angry or scared or sad or excited enough to do anything about their feelings. They may act as if there is nothing that can be done about the problem, or finally, they may discount their ability to deal with problems in general. Discounts must be confronted with caring so people will stop suffering and will deal with their problems.

HOW TO DEAL WITH DISCOUNTS

Discount	Confrontation
1. "There's nothing the matter." (discount of problem)	"How about you thinking about what you are feeling?" "I'm willing to talk to you about it if you want to." "It is not O.K. with me for you to discount your feelings. They are important and you can deal with your feelings or ask for help."
2. "Oh, it's not important; I'll probably feel better tomorrow." (discount of significance)	"Sounds like you are having some feelings that you are not dealing with." "Will you think about what you are feeling and talk to me about it?" "It's not O.K. with me for you to discount the importance of your feelings."
3. "Well, there is nothing that can be done anyway." (discount of solution)	"Sounds like it seems hopeless to you right now." "Will you think about what you are willing to do about your problem? Only if you have tried at least five options without success will I accept your definition that it is hopeless." "You can think effectively and solve problems."
4. "I don't know what to do, it's too much to think about." (self-discount)	"Sounds like you are feeling helpless about solving your problem." "You can think and feel at the same time and use both to solve your problem." "How about thinking about what you can do to solve the problem?"

Many students will not learn to think and solve problems unless you are willing to put energy into confronting passivity and discounting. Because the passive person must learn to think about what he or she wants or needs and how to get it, you must be sure that you don't support any of the passive behaviors. One of the most common ways that teachers support passivity is by rescuing, which is doing something for someone else that he or she could do for himself or herself. Some people who engage in rescuing use it to feel needed, to feel important, to gain control over another person, or to avoid dealing with their own problems.

ACTIVITY 21—TAKING RESPONSIBILITY[1]

Rationale: Many people have developed the habit of externalizing blame, of blaming someone else for problems. Children who are fearful of punishment will often try to present themselves as the innocent victim of another child's misbehavior.

When blaming becomes a way of thinking and behaving, it greatly inhibits your freedom and the amount of personal power and choice you have. By identifying and owning what you have done to create a problem, you can begin to take steps to either solve it or avoid a similar problem in the future. As long as you deny any responsibility for your problems, conflicts, or unhappiness, you are likely to feel helpless and hopeless or angry about the "mistreatment" you receive. You cannot really control what others do, whereas you *can* control and change what you do. By examining your responsibility in a situation, you can also benefit from the lesson inherent in it.

Step 1: Have the children get into groups of three.

Step 2: Each person in the triad is to think of a problem or conflict in which he or she felt mistreated or victimized. They are to take turns telling the other two in their group about this situation. Ask them to focus on what the other people did, i.e., how the other people mistreated them.

Step 3: Allow about five minutes per person. Circulate around the classroom as children tell each other their situations and make sure they are following your instructions.

Step 4: (See Step 5.) After each person in the triad has had his or her turn, instruct the children to tell each other their situations again, but this time, *they* are to take *full responsibility* for what happened. They should tell their situations from the point of view of what they did or did not do to create the problem or conflict and not blame at all the other people involved.

Step 5: You will probably need to discuss this step before doing Step 4. You are likely to encounter a lot of resistance to and argument about this

[1]Adapted from an exercise by Lynn C. Elliott, "Centering in Feeling and Communication," in eds. Gay Hendricks and Thomas B. Roberts, *The Second Centering Book* (Englewood Cliffs, N.J.: Prentice-Hall, Inc., 1977), pp. 109–11.

part of the activity. Ask the children to do Step 4 even though they may think their situations were other people's faults.

Step 6: Again, allow about five minutes per person and circulate around the classroom to see if your instructions are being followed.

Step 7: Ask the children to think about what they could have done differently in their situations to have avoided feeling bad or victimized or to have avoided the problem altogether. Ask them also to identify what lesson they would learn from their situations. What can they learn about themselves? Was there something familiar to them about their situation? Did they end up having some familiar feelings? Do they see any patterns in their behavior, the tendency to create similar situations or to have similar feelings? Ask for discussion of these questions.

Step 8: Discuss the activity and how the children felt as they did the two parts. Discuss what can be gained from taking responsibility for our behavior and our contribution to our problems or conflicts. Ask them what, if anything, is gained when we blame others and disown our responsibility.

To the Teacher: Many people (including adults) find this activity to be difficult and are resistant to it. It is also a powerful activity in which people can learn a tremendous amount and gain or regain much personal power.

To facilitate participants' understanding of the activity, you may want to begin by having three people demonstrate in front of the whole group.

ACTIVITY 22—THE RESCUE GAME[2]

Rationale: Rescuing occurs when you do something for someone, without being asked, that he or she could do for him- or herself. When you rescue, you discount the other person, and thus reinforce a position of passivity.

In order for there to be a "rescuer," there must be a "victim" who is being persecuted by a "persecutor." There are, of course, situations in which someone is in real physical danger, and it is healthy and appropriate to rescue. A drowning child is in fact in need of being rescued, and if

[2]*Ibid.*, pp. 129–31.

he or she isn't, the child may die. In most cases, however, rescuing is not healthy or appropriate and involves discounting and passivity.

Many of us have the mistaken notion that we are doing someone a favor when we rescue them, that we are helping them out, for instance, by "getting them off the hook." The opposite is true, however, because rescuing is treating the person as if he or she were helpless and incapable of acting effectively.

Step 1: Ask for three volunteers who would like to do some acting.

Step 2: One of the volunteers will play the role of a victim, acting helpless and incapable. One of the volunteers will play the role of persecutor, the "bad guy" who picks on the helpless victim. The other volunteer will play the role of the rescuer who takes care of the helpless victim.

Step 3: Describe a situation in which there is a rescuer, victim, and persecutor. You may be able to use one that has actually occurred in the classroom recently.

Step 4: Instruct the volunteers in their roles and have them act out their parts. (Make sure you do *not* pick a situation in which the victim really needs to be rescued, really is unable to take care of him- or herself.)

Step 5: With the whole group, discuss each volunteer's role. Was the victim *really* helpless? What could he or she have done? Did the victim really need to be rescued?

Step 6: Discuss how we sometimes play these roles in our lives and how people tend to have a favorite role. Do they ever play these roles? Which role do they usually play—rescuer, victim, or persecutor? Discuss the concepts of discounting and passivity and what kind goes on in each role.

To the Teacher: This activity is a simple way to introduce children to the concept of rescuing. The discussion, however, could take place over several days and involves some complex ideas and concepts.

It will be well worth your while to explain and discuss what discounting and passivity are and to establish no-discounting, no-passivity contracts in your classroom. This agreement will make your job easier in the long run and greatly improve the climate for learning and interpersonal relationships in your classes.

7

Straightening Out
the Maze

COOPERATION VERSUS COMPETITION

Cooperation between people is a way of relating interpersonally and is based upon the belief that both parties can get what they need or want, that they both can "win." By contrast, interpersonal competition is based on the assumptions that there isn't enough to go around and only one person can "win"; the other must "lose."

Interpersonal competition is rampant in our society, as individualism and capitalism are inherently competitive. It would be safe to say that everyone growing up and living in our society has absorbed and learned some competitive behaviors, which are then expressed in interpersonal relationships. How often are two people in a couple really equal? How common are power struggles and attempts to control another person? How often do two people work together cooperatively so that both get what they want and need a majority of the time?

There are definitely arenas in our lives where competition is straightforward and appropriate, such as in sports and games. In these situations the structure *is* one in which somebody wins the game or match and someone else loses, and both parties or teams have agreed to these conditions.

In interpersonal relationships, competition is inappropriate, unnecessary, and dysfunctional. When interpersonal competition occurs, one person is one up and the other is one down; one or both people are discounting themselves and/or each other, and there is no conscious, agreed-upon contract for these conditions. They promote discord and conflict and invite power plays, interpersonal games, and one-upmanship.

The opposite of interpersonal competition is interpersonal cooperation. Steiner (1974) has identified five conditions that must exist and be agreed upon for a cooperative relationship to be established and maintained:

1. *No scarcity.* There is enough for both people to get what they want and need most of the time. In some situations, there is a real scarcity. For instance, a husband may have to work overtime for a week and not be able or willing to engage in the social activities his wife requests he attend. In a cooperative situation, a compromise would be reached.

2. *Equal rights.* Given that both parties agree not to create scarcities, they also agree that they have equal rights to satisfying wants and needs and share equal responsibility for cooperating.

3. *No power plays.* Power plays include behaviors such as threatening, yelling, slamming out of the room, and discounting, all used in an attempt to get what you want.

4. *No secrets.* Both parties agree to ask for what they want 100 percent of the time rather than trying manipulation or power plays.

5. *No rescues.* Both parties agree that each of them is capable of asking for and getting what they want. Both agree not to do things for each other without being asked, not to do things they don't want to do just because the other wants it, and not to discount each other.

In competitive, individualistic situations people are trained to not say what they want because to express one's wants or needs will immediately decrease the supply of what is needed and create a scarcity. By contrast, in cooperative situations, to state what you want is required for satisfaction and is a first step in obtaining it.

A major area of interpersonal competition is in giving and receiving "strokes," or positive attention. The competitive stance is that if another person gets strokes and recognition, you won't, because there aren't enough strokes available for both of you. This kind of competition is very apparent in children. If one child sees a sibling getting attention, he or she will usually react by competing for that attention. This behavior is also observable in the classroom.

Cooperation can be fostered and taught in the classroom in a variety of ways. You must first believe and act on the belief that more than one person can fulfill wants and needs at a time. When one group of children wants to do one thing and another group wants to do something else, you can help to arrange for both groups to do what they want, perhaps at different times, or to reach a compromise. When two or more children want your attention, and the requests are reasonable and straightforward, you can let them know you will be with them in a minute. By giving a lot of positive strokes to all the children consistently, you can reduce or eliminate a great deal of competition, acting out, and fighting. When two children are arguing you can ask each to state how he or she feels and to ask for what is wanted from the other. They can either each change their behavior or reach a compromise.

COOPERATIVE PROBLEM SOLVING

Cooperative problem solving requires that several conditions exist.

1. The people involved must regard and treat each other as equals.
2. The people involved must be willing to own responsibility for their contribution to the problem. No one is the "bad guy"; there is no blaming.
3. Each person involved is 100 percent responsible for the problem and for solving it cooperatively.
4. The people involved must have an equal investment in solving the problem.
5. There must be no discounting or power plays.
6. The people involved agree to ask for what they want.

One way to approach cooperative problem solving is for one person to state what he or she perceives to be his or her part in the problem. This kind of beginning is effective in avoiding defensiveness on the part of the second person. After stating his or her perception of and contribution to the problem, the first person can then ask what the other person thinks or feels. Once both have agreed upon the definition of the problem and have owned their contribution, both can state what they are willing to do to solve the problem and/or to avoid its recurrence. Either party can also ask the other for anything else he or she wants.

An example of such an approach is as follows:

1st PERSON: I'm feeling like we've been distant with each other and I don't like that. My part in that is that I've really been worried about work and instead of talking to you about that, I've kind of withdrawn. What do you think?

2nd PERSON: I've been feeling distant, too. I guess when I saw you withdraw, I withdrew too. I don't like it either and I'd like us to be close.

1st PERSON: What I'm willing to do is to either leave work worries at work, or if that's really on my mind, I'll talk to you about it.

2nd PERSON: O.K. I'd like you to share that with me. What I'll do is if I see you withdraw, I'll ask you to talk to me instead of withdrawing. I'd also like us to spend more time together. I'd like to go out to dinner tomorrow night. Are you up for that?

1st PERSON: Yeah, let's do that.

ACTIVITY 23—HELPING KIDS SOLVE PROBLEMS COOPERATIVELY

Rationale: This approach to problem solving is also effective in helping people learn to take responsibility for their behavior, and avoids the problems created by laying blame. Most children have experienced the reaction of parents and teachers who look for someone to blame for misbehavior or for a problem. Thus, the children tend to be defensive and often try to put all the blame on someone else.

In teaching children how to solve problems cooperatively, you must make clear to them that one or both of them is not going to be blamed and punished, that what you want them to do is to solve the problem together. Many of them will never have experienced this kind of approach and so they will need reassurance and encouragement. You will also need to provide the structure for them, e.g., as in the following:

72

Step 1: Get the two children away from the group unless you can get the group to be quiet and listen to how the problem is solved.

Step 2: Ask the child who seems most upset to state what he or she thinks the problem is. Ask the other child to remain quiet; he or she will have a chance to talk in a minute. The first child should direct his or her statement to the other child, not to you (not using third-person pronouns).

Step 3. Ask the first child to think about how he or she has contributed to the problem. Do not allow blaming or accusing and let the child know that the other child will be asked what he or she did, too. The child may need a few minutes to think about this question. If he or she stubbornly refuses to take any ownership of the problem, have him or her sit alone quietly somewhere until he or she is ready to think. Do not allow the child to do other things until the problem is solved.

Step 4: After the first child has identified his or her part in the problem, follow the same process with the second child.

Step 5: Paraphrase what each has said and give them a lot of strokes for owning their parts in the problem.

Step 6: Ask both to think about what they could each do to solve the problem and to avoid it happening again. Then ask them to tell each other what they *will* do. Again, do not allow either to disown responsibility for solving the problem.

Step 7: Paraphrase what they have said and give them strokes for good thinking.

Step 8: Next ask each if either one wants something else from the other. If so, have him or her state what it is, and ask if the other is willing to do it. Make sure they both understand they can say yes or no.

Step 9: When they have finished, check to see if both are feeling good about the problem and if they think it has been solved. Give them a lot of strokes for solving the problem.

Step 10: If the whole group has watched this process, you can ask for discussion of what took place. Point out that problems *can* be solved, that blaming and accusing doesn't solve problems but creates more.

To the Teacher: The first few times you do this activity it will probably be fairly time-consuming. One way to make it easier is for you to model this approach when you and a child come into conflict. In the case of a child acting out when you have done nothing you're aware of to contribute to the problem, use the model suggested in Chapter 6 for expressing feelings effectively:

> I feel _____
> because _____.
> What I want from you is _____.
> Will you do that? If not, what are you willing to do?

It is important to invite the child to express his or her feelings, too. There is *some* reason for the acting out, which may or may not be connected to the here and now or to anything you have done or not done. However, in cooperative problem solving, both parties must be given the opportunity to express their feelings and to ask for what they want. This situation also provides the opportunity to reinforce cooperative, responsible behavior. Take every opportunity possible to verbally reward such behavior.

SKILLS IN MAKING CONTRACTS

Contracts can be an effective tool for developing effective interpersonal communication because (1) they spell out rules or behavioral limits, (2) they make expectations clear, (3) they allow students to question and understand the rules and expectations, (4) they set up a structure in which there is mutual responsibility in enforcing the conditions of the contracts. Contracts also may be used as a way to deal with problem behavior.

Contracts need not always be written. If you would like the entire group to agree to solve problems cooperatively as outlined above, you can simply ask if everyone agrees to do that. It is important to insure that all the children understand what they are agreeing to and that you get a verbal "yes" or "no" to the question.

Following is an example of a contract that deals with problem behavior (an example of a learning contract can be found in Chapter 12):

I, _____, understand that talking out of turn or to my neigh-
   (student's name)
bors is not a very effective way of getting attention and disturbs other people. I agree to raise my hand when I want to talk.

I, _____, understand that you have trouble sitting in your seat
   (teacher)
quietly for long periods of time. I agree to provide breaks in school work when it is O.K. to talk to other kids and to walk around. I also agree to call on you as soon as I can when you raise your hand.

_____	_____
(date)	(student)
_____	_____
	(teacher)

Such a contract could be arrived at after you and a student have gone through the process of cooperative problem solving and can be used as a way to prevent the reoccurrence of a similar problem. It is important that all parties have input into any contract and have the opportunity to identify and state what they will do and what they want from others.

SKILLS IN CONFRONTATION

In confronting behavior in others, use all the skills discussed in this section, including the communication guidelines. Of particular importance is owning your own feelings, thoughts, or opinions by saying, "I think . . ." or "I feel . . ." etc., and avoid accusations, interpretations, or demands. Following are some examples of ways to confront effectively, with caring:

"I feel discounted because you just interrupted me. Will you stop doing that, please?"

(Child comes home late after having agreed to be on time) "We had an agreement that you would be home on time and you're a half hour late. I expect you to do what you say you will do and to be home on time. If you're going to be late and can't make it on time, I want you to call me. Will you do that?"

To confront effectively, you need to communicate clearly and specifically and to avoid aggravating the situation by putting the other person on the defensive. When confrontations are straightforward and caring, everyone has the right to confront, and as they exercise that right, confrontations lose their threat.

Confrontation is a sign of caring and should be presented as such. If I am indifferent to someone, I do not bother to confront his or her behavior.

Three rules of thumb are suggested in order to decide whether to confront or not:

1. Confront behavior when you want to be closer to someone. Caring, effective confrontation results in both people getting to know each other better and in sharing feelings.
2. Confront when someone's behavior is affecting you adversely in some important way.
3. Confront the inappropriate behavior of someone for whom you have some responsibility (a child) or when you have a contract to do so (such as in a therapist–client relationship).

8

Becoming Real

SELF-DISCLOSURE AND MODELING SKILLS

Self-disclosure occurs when you share your feelings, thoughts, and reactions to the present situation as well as the past, which is related to how you are responding in the present. It isn't necessary to share every intimate detail of your past to be self-disclosing. A person gets to know you by how you react to situations, to other people, and to him or her.

The degree to which you are self-disclosing determines in large part how close a relationship will be. It is not possible to have a really close relationship unless both people are willing to be honest and to share their inner feelings with each other.

Self-disclosure involves taking risks. You are taking the chance of letting someone else know you, perhaps understand you, and you therefore take the risk that they may not like you, may judge you in some way or reject you. It is only common sense, therefore, to choose people you trust and with whom you feel comfortable and to adjust your self-disclosure according to how much you trust and how close you want to be.

The person who refuses to self-disclose with anyone or who is dishonest in self-disclosures is a very lonely person. Particularly in times of stress, we seem to need to be able to talk openly and honestly about how we are feeling and what we are thinking.

Your ability to be self-disclosing depends upon your self-awareness. You must be in touch with your own feelings to be able to share them with others. The degree to which you are comfortable with and accepting of yourself also affects self-disclosure. If you do not accept your own feelings it is unlikely that you will be willing to share them with anyone else.

To form a close relationship you must also be willing and able to listen to the other person's self-disclosure. The more accepting and supportive you are of the other person, the more he or she will feel comfortable in sharing with you.

Giving people information about how we feel about them and how we react to their behavior is often referred to as feedback. Feedback can be helpful and productive or it can be threatening and nonproductive. Before offering feedback, it is useful to be sure the person wants to hear what you have to say. Perhaps the other person asks for some feedback, or you can say something like, "I've got some feedback for you. Do you want to hear it?"

Your feedback to people will be the most productive and least threatening when you follow these guidelines:

1. Offer feedback about the person's behavior rather than about the person.
2. Make your feedback as specific as possible, related to the person's current behavior.
3. Offer feedback that has value and relevance for the person and can be used by him or her. Feedback is for the other person, not for you.
4. Avoid interpreting, assigning motives, and giving advice.

There are times when you will want to tell people something about your reactions to them that is not necessarily based on the value and relevance it has to *them*, but rather on its value and relevance to *you*. Not what is normally termed "feedback," although it may serve the same function, this is more of a confrontation.

ACTIVITY 24—HOW SELF-DISCLOSING AM I?

Rationale: A popular, beginning exercise in self-disclosure is the Johari Window, developed by Luft and Ingham.[1] This device gives people an opportunity to examine how self-disclosing they are as well as how self-aware.

The Johari Window consists of a square divided into four parts, as shown in Figure 4.

	KNOWN TO SELF	UNKNOWN TO SELF
KNOWN TO OTHERS	FREE TO SELF AND OTHERS 1	BLIND TO SELF AND SEEN BY OTHERS 2
UNKNOWN TO OTHERS	HIDDEN: SELF HIDDEN FROM OTHERS 3	UNKNOWN: SELF UNKNOWN TO OTHERS AND SELF 4

Figure 4.

Step 1: Mimeograph sheets with this diagram at the top and an empty square to be filled in by participants at the bottom.

Step 2: Pass the sheets out to all participants. Explain the diagram at the top of the sheet and discuss briefly what self-disclosure is.

Step 3: Ask each participant to divide the empty square on their sheets according to how they see themselves. Explain that everyone's window will be a little different. On the blackboard, draw a couple of windows and explain what each means. For instance, the window shown in Figure 5 reflects a person who is very self-disclosing and self-aware.

Figure 6 shows other variations. Ask the children to identify the meaning of each example.

Step 4: After all the participants have completed their own windows,

[1]Joe Luft, *Of Human Interaction* (Palo Alto, Cal.: National Press, 1969).

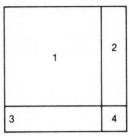

Figure 5.

have them get into small groups or pairs and discuss them. Ask them to talk about what they keep hidden from others but know themselves. What do they think others see in them that they don't see? How much of them is unknown to themselves and to others? How open are they to others, generally? What are some reasons why we sometimes hide parts of our personalities from others?

Step 5: Discuss the relationship between self-disclosure and closeness with others. At the beginning of a relationship, how much does the other person know about us? What would the window look like? When we have developed a close relationship, how would the window change?

To the Teacher: A variation of this exercise is to ask participants to discuss their windows with a close friend and get feedback about how the friend sees their self-disclosure and self-awareness. Another variation is to have participants do the exercise in pairs, each person drawing a window for himself and for his partner; then they discuss similarities and differences in how they see themselves and each other.

Another interesting exercise is to see how your window changes over time, especially after going through some training in interpersonal skills or self-awareness.

ACTIVITY 25—FEEDBACK

Rationale: An excellent way to deal with conflict in a group or between two people is to give feedback to each other. This activity needs to be structured, with ground rules, to avoid arguments or negative feelings.

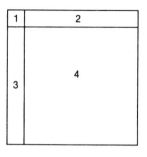

OR

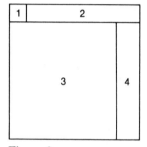

Figure 6.

Step 1: Explain what feedback is. If the group is very large, divide it into two or three groups, providing you have enough people to help each group.

Step 2: Set the following ground rules:

1. One person speaks at a time (you may want them to raise their hands for recognition).
2. No shouting, swearing, or denigrating remarks are allowed.
3. No one is to leave the group until the exercise is over.
4. The person receiving feedback may only ask for clarification if he or she doesn't understand what has been said. He or she may not defend or argue.

Step 3: Depending upon your purpose, you can have people either ask for feedback from others or give it to specific people. You can also structure this as a "strength-building" exercise in which only positive feedback is given. You can ask participants to give feedback about what they don't like about each other's behavior, or you can allow both positive and negative feedback.

Decide upon the structure you want and explain it to the group.

Step 4: Begin the feedback. A half hour to an hour is the optimal time for this exercise with children.

Step 5: Before discussing the activity, check with each participant, especially any member(s) who have received negative feedback. Make sure no one is going away with hurt or angry feelings.

Step 6: Discuss how this exercise was for the participants. Was it hard or scary to get feedback? What did they learn about themselves or others? Did anyone think they were being criticized? What is the difference between criticism and feedback?

To the Teacher: To resolve conflicts a variation of this activity is to incorporate the cooperative problem-solving structure suggested in Chapter 7. Another possibility is to structure the group so that each person expresses how he or she feels about another's behavior and asks for what he or she wants from that person. ("I feel _____ because/about _____. What I want from you is _____. Will you do that?")

It is very important that you structure this group, lay down ground rules, and make sure participants follow them. Without such structure, this can be a negative, destructive process.

GETTING WANTS AND NEEDS MET EFFECTIVELY

In previous chapters, we have discussed how to become aware of wants and needs, viewing feelings as a source of self-information and using the energy generated by feelings to solve problems. There are several other pitfalls in communication as well as effective strategies to be used.

To simply identify and verbalize what you want or need is not enough. You must also ask if the other person is willing to do as you want. If I say, "I want you to help with the housework," and do not follow that statement with a request, I am inviting other people either to rescue me and do something they have not been asked to do, or to discount and ignore what I've said because I didn't ask them for anything. To get wants and needs met effectively you must be active in asking for them.

If you are to be successful in getting what you want a majority of the time, you must also pay attention to the realities of a situation and what others have to offer. Pursuing a close relationship with someone who is guarded and defensive probably will result in not getting what you want. If I discount the fact that my boss is busy and feeling pressured and try to talk to him about an important concern of mine, I am likely to not get the response I want. If I decide I want to achieve something and unrealistically discount the limitations of my abilities, I may set myself up to fail.

Passivity and competition also get in the way of effective behavior. If you are passive and expect someone else to take care of you, you will probably be disappointed. If you believe that "there isn't enough to go around" and assume that you cannot get what you want in a straightforward manner—that you have to connive and manipulate—you may get what you want but probably at the expense of incurring resentment, dislike, or rejection from others. Similarly, the competitive position that only one person can win, that one person must be one up and the other one down, tends to be highly dysfunctional. If you take the one-up position, others will eventually resent you. If you take the one-down position, you are going to set up situations so that you reinforce and maintain that pattern.

Effectively getting wants and needs met requires that you pay attention to all aspects of the situation, including your feelings, wants, needs, abilities; the other person's feelings, wants, needs, and abilities; and the realities of the external situation. It also requires a willingness to actively take responsibility for yourself.

9

My Values
Are Better Than Yours

SKILLS IN CLARIFYING VALUES

All of us have attitudes, beliefs, opinions, and values upon which we base decisions and create life styles. We develop our value systems in a variety of ways from a variety of sources.

One of the problems facing young people in this country today is that there is such a variety of value systems. Parents have one set, churches another, their peer group and educational system still others; plus they are exposed to a variety of other cultural and subcultural value systems through the media. Children often react to this variety by experiencing a lot of confusion and conflict or by dogmatically adopting and maintaining one particular set of values.

Compounding this confusion is the fact that many adults try to impose their value system on children, focusing on the *content* of values. Just as the public school tends to emphasize the teaching of content rather than the process of learning, children tend to be inundated with specific values. This method creates the additional conflict of forcing a child to either accept or reject any given value, instead of equipping him or her with the skills necessary to develop a value system. We tend to teach children the content of values, rather than the *process* of valuing.

Thus many, if not most, children develop their value systems unconsciously rather than by conscious decision or choice; and until their values become conscious, they cannot examine or consider them.

Raths suggests that valuing consists of seven subprocesses:

prizing one's beliefs and behaviors
   1. prizing and cherishing
   2. publicly affirming, when appropriate

choosing one's beliefs and behaviors
   3. choosing from alternatives
   4. choosing after consideration of consequences
   5. choosing freely

acting on one's beliefs
   6. acting
   7. acting with a pattern, consistency, and repetition[1]

The approach developed by Simon, Howe, and Kirschenbaum (1972) teaches the valuing process and helps people make conscious value choices. Their book contains over fifty exercises and activities designed to help young people identify, examine, and clarify their values.

HOW TO DEAL EFFECTIVELY WITH VALUES

Much interpersonal conflict revolves around different value systems and the position that one set of values is "right" and another is "wrong." This conflict covers the range from the minor squabbles of children to international wars.

Often, along with the assumption that a set of values is right is the conclusion that it is all right or even necessary to impose those values on others. This belief involves a grave discount of individuals' right to choose and their ability to act with integrity.

One of the most valuable skills you can teach children is that of respecting their own and others' values, as well as the awareness that values are a matter of choice. Values often incorporate beliefs or decisions about what

[1]Louis Raths, Merrill Harmon, Sidney Simon, *Values and Teaching* (Columbus, Ohio: Charles E. Merrill, 1966).

is right or wrong. However, these are personal, individual decisions and do not automatically rule out the possibility that someone else's values may be just as "right."

Responsible valuing involves a willingness to accept the consequences of holding one's values and acting in accordance with them. If I do not value human life and kill someone, I must be willing to accept the imprisonment or death sentence this society imposes for such behavior. If I do not care about other people's feelings and treat people cruelly, with insensitivity, I should be prepared to be rejected and disliked by many.

ACTIVITY 26—EXPERIENCING OTHERS' VALUES

Rationale: Values are also developed as a result of your experiences, culture or subculture, and the way in which you have been raised. The specific design of this activity will depend upon the backgrounds of the children in your classroom. The goals of this activity are to help children realize (1) that values are a matter of choice; (2) that people's values are related to their life experiences; (3) that there are not *right* and *wrong* values, but there are *different* values.

Following is an example of how this activity might be designed for use with children of white, middle-class background. This activity will be most effective if preceeded by some of the exercises in Simon *et al*. (1972).

Step 1: List on the blackboard some of the values the group shares about a particular subject or subjects, such as "What is success?"

Step 2: Ask them to imagine that they grew up on small farms in very poor families. Describe some of the particulars in this life style: they have to get up at four or five in the morning to do chores, milk the cow, collect eggs; they walk miles to school; most of their clothes are handed down from older brothers or sisters; their mothers and fathers work hard on the farm all day; sometimes they have very little to eat; etc.

Step 3: Ask them what values this background might instill, and list these on the board.

Step 4: Discuss the differences in the two lists. Is one set of values "right," the other "wrong?" Have they known people who have had very different values than they?

To the Teacher: This activity can be used many times and is a good way for children to learn about different cultures or subcultures, as well as an effective way to help them understand valuing. You can get into very controversial issues with older students or adults, such as the values that underlie criminal behavior, different religious and political beliefs, etc.

10

Teacher, May I?

WHAT ARE PERMISSIONS?

Permissions are positive messages available from yourself, other people, and your environment that support your positive changes. Permissions exist everywhere and are always available if you know how to find them.

What makes it difficult for you to see the permissions available to you are the decisions you made early in your life about how you are going to view yourself, other people, and the world around you. These decisions form your script, or life plan, which you act upon in everything you do and say. Your script tends to narrow or limit your perceptions of yourself, other people, and your environment to those things that support it and your decisions.

YOUR SCRIPT DECISIONS

Following is a chart showing the eleven most common script decisions that most people make before they reach adulthood.[1] Also included are some common perceptions that are related to each decision.

[1] Barry K. Weinhold and Gail Andresen, *Threads! Unraveling the Mysteries of Adult Life* (New York: Richard Marek Publishers, 1979).

Decision	*Common Perceptions*
I won't exist	I don't belong, others don't think I'm worth much, I am a bother to other people. There's nothing in the world for me.
I won't be the sex I am	I can't succeed as a (boy or girl); I wish I were a (the opposite sex); Others don't like me as a (boy or girl). My parents wanted a (boy or girl) *instead of me.*
I won't be a child	I have to "act grown-up" for people to like me; I have to suffer to get others to take care of me; life isn't much fun.
I won't have needs of my own	I have to take care of others to get them to take care of me; I'm not worthy of asking for what I want; I have to do what others want me to *do in order to be accepted.*
I won't think	I am dumb, stupid; if I act confused someone will think for me; I'll let others (parents, teachers) make decisions for me.
I won't feel	It's not safe to show feelings; my feelings are so powerful they can control me. I'll let others tell me what I should feel.
I won't get close	If people get close to me they will reject me; I won't know what to do if I get close; people who want to get close to me are going to hurt me.
I won't grow up	Growing up means not having fun; growing up requires too much responsibility on my part; others will take care of me if I act like a child.
I won't succeed	There is no reward for doing things successfully; I can't meet other people's expectations so why try.
I won't be sane	If I act crazy, people will pay attention to me; I'm different from other people; I can scare other people.
I won't	The world is a dangerous place; you can get into trouble if you ask too many questions; I can't do many things without getting hurt.

According to permission theory, you can identify your own childhood decisions and then learn the skills and techniques necessary to change the old decisions into new ones. The following self-survey may help you identify these decisions and their possible effects.[2]

[2]*Ibid.*, p. 62.

SELF-SURVEY ON SCRIPT DECISIONS

Decision Perceptions   *Frequency of Perception*

	Hardly Ever	Sometimes	Usually	Most of the Time
1. I don't believe I'm very worthwhile or important as a person.				
2. I wish I were a person of a different sex.				
3. I have trouble really "letting go" and having fun.				
4. I have a hard time putting my needs and wants first.				
5. When faced with a problem to solve, I get confused and don't know what to do.				
6. I don't seem to be able to know when I'm feeling sad, mad, scared, or glad.				
7. I don't seem to be able to get close to people when I want to.				
8. I find it hard to deal with life's responsibilities.				
9. I have trouble finishing projects after I get started.				
10. Things I say and do seem "crazy" to others.				
11. I seem to have difficulty when I try something for the first time.				
12. I don't take the risk of trying new things.				

_____ + _____ + _____ + _____ = _____

Total Score

SCORING PROCEDURES

Each item is scored 1 = Hardly ever, 2 = Sometimes, 3 = Usually, and 4 = Most of the time. Write a number in the column where you placed a check mark, and add all the numbers in each column to get your score. Place your score on the continuum below and look at the suggested interpretation.

11	22	44

INTERPRETATION

11–16	absence of major restrictive decisions
17–22	some early script decisions may be affecting your life
23–28	most early script decisions may be affecting your life
29–34	you seem to be not enjoying your life very much
35+	you may be leading a restricted life

THE DYNAMICS OF CHANGING YOUR DECISIONS

Script decisions are usually made before the age of sixteen and are a form of adaptation to your particular life during childhood and adolescence. Generally there are three conditions that were present when the original decision was made. First, you probably were under some form of duress and pressure. That is, you perceived your parents or others as putting some pressure on you to behave in a certain way or they would not accept or like you. Whether or not they actually did threaten to reject you isn't important. The important issue is what you decided about yourself, others, and the world around you. Most children use the information they get from their parents and other adults. Sometimes this information is sufficient, but often it isn't or it is distorted by the child's interpretation. For example, a parent in a frustrated moment may say to a child, "You are driving me crazy." With this kind of information a child can make a variety of decisions depending on his or her interpretation.

Finally, these decisions were almost always made while you were still dependent on your parents in important ways, which limited the number of options you may have had. Financial dependence, for example, severely limits choices. Very often the choices that are open involve staying in the situation and acting powerless.

The decisions themselves are often feeble attempts to get even from a powerless position, and the best way to do so is to make it all someone else's fault. What happens is that when people become adults they are no longer under duress, they have access to more information, and they are more independent financially and emotionally. However, if they haven't change. Others remember an influential book, movie, or television show, and still others report finding some internal voice that seemed to say, "Yes, you can do it." All of these are important sources of permission, and they are always present for us to use if we choose.

In order for you to change your decisions, you first have to stop trying to blame your parents or others for not giving you everything you wanted but never got. No parent, teacher, or other adult can ever provide enough love, information, support, caring, etc., that you may have needed or wanted. The whole set of expectations you developed is part of the unreasonable demands that society places on parents and teachers. You probably learned this system well and learned to push on the "guilty buttons" of your parents to get what you wanted.

If you haven't changed your basic decisions, as adults you probably are still pushing on the "guilty buttons" of others in hopes of making them guilty enough to give you what you want. What is obvious about that position is that it is still powerless, relying on the power of others instead of your own. So in order to change your decisions, you must first decide to give up blaming your parents and others and put your energy into learning more effective ways to get what you want.

There seems to be a number of factors involved in making this initial switch in energy. Usually people report the influence of a particular teacher, minister, counselor, or friend, who gave them the permission to change. Others remember an influential book, movie, or television show, and still others report finding some internal voice that seemed to say, "Yes, you can do it." All of these are important sources of permission, and they are always present for us to use if we choose.

As teachers and counselors you see children and adolescents all the time who have made limiting decisions about themselves. You are often in a good position to provide the necessary permission for them to begin to change these decisions.

The first step in the permission process is the use of good interpersonal communication skills, which allow yourself to be seen by your students as someone worth their attention. Students bestow a kind of natural authority on parents, teachers, and other adults who respond genuinely and openly as a person and don't hide behind their role for an artificial authority.

Young people are used to being responded to by adults as if they were irresponsible, incompetent, ignorant, foolish, and not very important. If you treat young people with respect, generally you will get back respect—even though at first some of them may test your sincerity.

The actual permissions cannot be reduced to any formula or step-by-step procedure. Permissions are whatever you say and do that communicates to another person respect and support for their efforts to change.

PERMISSION ACTIVITIES

The following activities are designed to help you and your students begin to identify limiting decisions and create awarenesses of possible changes.

ACTIVITY 27—PERMISSION CHECKLIST

Rationale: This checklist can be reproduced and given out to your students as a way of identifying possible permissions that they want and need. This checklist is a way to begin creating an attitude of self-assessment.

Step 1: Have your students fill out the following permission checklist:

Look at each of the following messages of permission and place a check mark beside those you believe would be helpful for you to remember and use in your everyday life.

_____ You are important.

_____ You can take your time.

93

_____ You can relax.

_____ You can make mistakes.

_____ You can play and have fun.

_____ You are fine just the way you are.

_____ You can be successful.

_____ You can ask for what you want and need.

_____ You can come first.

_____ You can be spontaneous and creative.

_____ You can take care of yourself.

_____ You can enjoy what you are doing.

_____ You can change yourself if you want to.

_____ You can _____. [fill in your own]

Step 2: Divide your students into groups of six to eight and have them share their lists with each other.

Step 3: Ask each student to select at least one of the messages he or she checked.

Step 4: Each student is instructed to ask the members of the group for the permission he or she wants. Tell them to ask, "Will you give me permission to _____?"

Step 5: Ask each other member of the group to reply with the permission requested. Also ask the group to monitor any verbal or nonverbal discounting of the permission, such as breaking eye contact or adding qualifiers like "I can't always be successful." Tell them to point out any discounts they observe.

To the Teacher: You may tally the number of permissions checked and make posters containing those that most students selected. Having the posters in the room as reminders is often enough to have a student give herself or himself the needed permission or ask for it from others.

ACTIVITY 28—PUT-DOWNS AND PERMISSIONS

Rationale: The purpose of this activity is to help you and your students identify the negative messages that are still affecting your lives and to discover the messages of permission you want or need.

Step 1: Ask your students to list as many negative messages as they can remember getting from peers, parents, teachers, or other adults. These are the things that people said to them that hurt their feelings or that they believe had some negative effects. Have them write them as they remembered them or experienced them. Examples might be, "Do as you're told," "Don't ask so many questions."

Step 2: Have them look over their lists to see how many of these messages are still having some negative effects. For example, the message, "You never do anything right," may have the following effect: "I won't try anything new unless I am sure I'll be good at it." Ask the students to write down the current effects of the messages they listed in Step 1.

Step 3: Now ask them to make a list of things they wish that others would have said to them, the positive things they believe would have helped them—for examples, "You're neat," "You think really well." This list represents the permissions that they still want and/or need.

Step 4: Divide your students into subgroups of six to eight. Ask them to share their three lists and to focus on developing a plan to get the permissions they still want or need. Ask them to report to the group in the following way: "I still want permission to _____ and what I'm going to do to get that permission is _____." Ask group members to give feedback on each student's plan.

To the Teacher: You may ask each student to write out his or her plan so you can read it and give feedback. This step is a check against someone designing a plan that is set up to fail in order to support a script position of "You can't get what you want." Also the first part of this activity may let resentments toward parents and others surface. There are some appropriate activities for forgiveness in Chapter 16 under unconditional love that would be useful follow-up activities for your students.

ACTIVITY 29—PERMISSION TELEGRAM

Rationale: Learning how to give yourself the permissions you want and need is a powerful tool. It means that you have given up the illusion that someone else is responsible for you.

Step 1: Have your students write a telegram to themselves using twenty-five words or less. The telegram should contain a permission to do something they want to do or a permission they have identified as important for them to remember.

Step 2: Ask them to read the telegram to themselves and write down any reactions that would indicate resistance to believing it, for example, "You are intelligent and can think really well [telegram]; but you can't figure out your math sometimes [resistance]."

Step 3: Then ask them to write another permission telegram that would change the resistance into a permission, for example, ". . . but you can't figure out your math sometimes" becomes, "you can ask for help with your math when you are stuck. Being intelligent also means asking for what you want and need." Again tell them to write down any resistance.

Step 4: Finally, after they have cleared away the resistance and can write their permission telegrams without it, have them share their experiences in a small group or with the whole class.

To the Teacher: This can be a powerful clearing exercise and can help your students learn a process of dealing with their own resistances. Some may need additional help at first in learning this important tool. Give them permission to ask for any assistance they want or need.

Also, consult Chapter 12 for more examples of how to use permissions in the regular curriculum.

Pardon My Relationships

SELF-SURVEY ON INTERPERSONAL PROCESSES

This instrument can be completed prior to beginning work on interpersonal communication skills to help identify where to begin or it can be used as a follow-up instrument to support the progress you have made. No matter how you choose to use the self-survey, please be honest with yourself when you fill it out or it will not have much value.

Directions: Place a check mark in the column that best represents your perception of yourself. Please answer every item.

	Never	Sometimes	Usually	Always
1. I check out what I think someone has said to me on a regular basis.				
2. I own and personalize what I say by saying "I feel" or "I think."				
3. I have a tendency to rescue people.				
4. I avoid discounting myself or others.				

	Never	Sometimes	Usually	Always
5. I ask for what I want.				
6. I confuse thinking and feeling.				
7. I avoid confronting others because I'm not perfect.				
8. I misinterpret and misunderstand others' verbal and nonverbal communication.				
9. I am aware of my nonverbal behavior and body language.				
10. My verbal and nonverbal messages are congruent.				
11. I am uncomfortable maintaining eye-contact when I talk to someone.				
12. I am able to express how I feel effectively.				
13. I don't think it's right to ask for what I want. If someone wants to give me something or do something for me, that's O.K. but I won't ask.				
14. I use my feelings as a source of self-information.				
15. I can't stand to see anyone cry or be sad.				
16. I confuse my feelings and have difficulty figuring out how I feel.				
17. I avoid being passive and actively take responsibility for myself and my behavior.				
18. I feel one up with some people and one down with others.				
19. I would rather avoid a problem than face it or try to solve it.				
20. I am honest and open and willing to disclose myself.				

_____ + _____ + _____ + _____ = _____

Total
Score

SCORING PROCEDURES

Each item is weighted 1, 2, 3, or 4. Certain items are keyed with the "Always" column, weighted at 4, and others with the "Never" column, weighted at 4. The following key shows how to score each item:

Items scored 1, 2, 3, 4 (Never = 1 and Always = 4) include numbers 1, 2, 4, 5, 9, 10, 12, 14, 17, and 20.

Items scored 4, 3, 2, 1 (Never = 4 and Always = 1) include numbers 3, 6, 7, 8, 11, 13, 15, 16, 18, and 19.

Write the appropriate number in the column where you placed a check mark. Add all the numbers in each column and add the sums of each column to get a total score. Place your score on the continuum below and look at the interpretation that fits your category.

20	50	80

20– 29 premature hardening of the categories

30–39 you've only just begun

40–49 limited awareness of interpersonal processes

50–59 review and sharpen your skills

60–69 high level of interpersonal awareness

70+ interpersonal go-getter

COMMON ERRORS IN
INTERPERSONAL COMMUNICATION

1. Saying "one" or "people" or "you" in expressing your point of view.
2. Asking a question instead of making a statement: "Don't you think that . . . ?"
3. Saying "I feel" to mean "I think."
4. Making a statement instead of asking for what you want or need, e.g., "I wish you were going into town."
5. In a group talking about a person and not to him.
6. Using "I can't" to mean "I won't" or "I don't want to."
7. Using "have to's" and "should's" when you mean you "choose to" or "want to."

8. Not answering a question directly: "How do you feel today?" Answer: "Why do you want to know?"

9. Using words like "I guess," "I think," or "maybe" when you are sure.

10. Using "try" instead of "do."

11. Blaming your feelings on someone else.

12. Confusing inference and observation.

13. Interrupting someone when he is speaking, which usually means you aren't listening.

14. Changing the subject or "chaining," i.e., listening to just enough of what someone says to change the subject to something you know more about or want to talk about.

15. Using statements like "always" or "never" to support your point of view.

16. Confusing feedback with confrontation.

17. Rescuing by doing something for someone that he or she can do for him or herself.

18. Making judgments about a person instead of offering feedback about behavior.

19. Discounting some aspect of a situation.

20. Maintaining a position of passivity instead of actively taking responsibility for yourself and your behavior.

21. Operating from a competitive framework in which you set up win or lose, one-up or one-down situations or relationships instead of cooperating as equals.

12

How to Integrate Interpersonal Communication Skills into the Regular Curriculum

This chapter contains four examples of how to teach various subjects in the regular curriculum by using some of the interpersonal communication skills presented in Chapters 6 through 10. We encourage you to adapt our examples to fit your classroom and to develop similar activities for using interpersonal skills in teaching.

TEACHING READING IN THE PRIMARY GRADES BY USING PERMISSIONS

The teaching of reading is a highly controversial subject in education with many strong, divergent views. Phonics, the international alphabet, formal programmed instruction such as Dystar, canned reading programs, informal developmental methods are a few of the diverse approaches to teaching reading. All of them try to convince children that reading is fun and easy and they'll like it. However, almost everything we say and do about reading carries hidden messages that are quite different. Parents, teachers, the government, and the whole society seem to be saying two things to children: "If we don't make you read, you lazy person, you never will learn to read," and "Reading is very difficult and complicated and you are so dumb that unless we break it down into tiny steps and lead you through it one step at a time, you won't be able to learn."

A testable hypothesis is, *most children teach themselves to read.* It may even take them longer if they have to overcome the interference that premature reading instruction has created. It is interesting that no one, to our knowledge, has tried to find out how many children do teach themselves to read. In response to the question, "How did you learn to read," one third-grade student said, "I just practiced. I wanted to know what all those words in books meant." It is true that children teach themselves far more complex things than reading. Television programs like "Sesame Street" and "The Electric Company" teach reading in a structured but informal way, using skits and dialogue to focus on various word concepts and sounds. The combination of sensory modalities, like visual and auditory ones, is useful.

Purpose: A permissions approach to reading conveys the message that reading is a natural process that doesn't require "special" attention, and that everyone can learn to read if and when he or she wants to. This approach emphasizes the importance of developing internal motivation so that reading takes place only when children think it's important and valuable to them.

Another important part of this approach is to make available positive support for reading from the child's environment (classroom, playground, neighborhood, and home); from significant others (teachers, parents, peers); and from the child himself or herself. In this more indirect approach, teachers are asked to integrate reading into the natural flow of the day's activities.

Procedures: These procedures are divided into three areas: first, those for creating a supportive environment with permission for learning to read; second, those for providing supportive permission by teachers, parents, and peers; and finally, those for helping children learn to use self-permissions.

Creating an environment for permission involves a number of activities. First, provide large posters that support learning to read. The International Reading Association provides some good ones, and you can make some yourself. They should contain positive messages to children about reading: "You Can Read Well," "You Can Learn to Read When You Want To," "Reading Can Be Fun," etc. Also, include pictures of children reading, and have plenty of books available around the room. Reading corners or enclosed areas where children can go to read are sometimes helpful too. Children can be taught to make their own supportive posters by cutting out words they like from magazines and newspapers. Use volunteers to help children with questions, like "What does this say?" If possible, have cassette tapes made of all the books available in the classroom so a child can listen to a tape while reading the story. Encourage children to make their own tapes so they may hear themselves reading. Have children make up their own stories, tape them, and then play them back.

In general, you want to communicate that you expect children to learn to read when they are ready and that it is no "big deal," just a natural process. If a child is trying too hard, you may have to give permission to that child to relax and do something else for a period of time. It is important to include parents in this process, as they can provide considerable support if given some instruction in how to facilitate these objectives.

Permissions from others is the next set of procedures to be described. As a teacher, you are in a crucial position to provide support and encouragement through the use of permissions. Your most important permissions convey to children that they are lovable and capable as people and that they can learn (to read) if they want to. Also, your permissions must support the idea that their sense of well-being and valuing comes from within themselves, not from you or others. For this reason, praise needs to be handled carefully. For example, instead of saying, "that is a good job of reading," focus on the child's internal frame of reference by saying something like, "You really like reading, don't you?" or "You seem pleased with yourself for reading that book." You may want to add to the latter response, ". . . and so am I," which still leaves internal permission or support as the primary response. In giving permissions, focus as much as possible on the child's internal thoughts and feelings. Children will provide many opportunities to give that kind of permission.

Self-permissions can be taught as a natural outgrowth of the above process. When children come to you for permissions you can remind them to give themselves permission too (Example: "You look like you are having fun with reading. Remember to give yourself permission to have fun while you are reading.")

One activity used successfully by several teachers is to have children make a cassette tape to play when they need or want to hear their permissions. The instructions are, "Say something you know you can do (in reading) that you want to remember," for examples, "I can read big words like 'happiness' " or "I can read a whole sentence without stopping" or "I can read a book every day, if I want to." Ask children to add new ones whenever they want, or suggest a schedule, like once a day or once a week. One teacher asked her third grade to make a thirty-second radio commercial of themselves and put it on tape. All these activities need to focus on the development of a positive self-image and success in whatever the child is doing, not just in learning to read.

PERMISSION ACTIVITY

Have the children sit in a circle and each select a book, poster, or something he or she can read. Establish some ground rules, such as only one person may speak at a time; there will be no disparaging remarks; everyone listens and may be asked to repeat what someone else has said. You direct the sessions and demonstrate the specific responses for which you are looking. The focus of the sessions is positive support of self-awareness of assets and strengths. Each child takes a turn reading one word (or one sentence or paragraph depending on the child's reading level). After reading the word, the child says to the group, "I can read the word _____." You as the teacher say something to support this achievement: "Yes, you can read the word _____." Repeat this process by going around the circle in turn. After every four or five children have recited say, "Who remembers who read the word _____?" Call on someone who might say, "Jimmy read the word _____." Compliment the person for remembering the other person's word.

Another way to achieve similar results is to ask periodically, "Can Jimmy read the word _____?" This method also provides children with permission messages that tell them they are effective and worthy. Periodically, ask children how they feel, perhaps by asking each child to complete the sentence, "I feel good about myself when _____." This method can generalize the good feelings in reading into other areas as well.

TEACHING SOCIAL STUDIES IN THE
INTERMEDIATE GRADES BY USING VALUES

The use of skills in clarifying values requires you, as a teacher, to use three levels of teaching: fact, concept, and value. With facts, you will help students learn various pieces of information—like dates, events, vocabulary—or basic skills such as reading or writing. At the level of concepts, you would help the student group various facts together to discover how concepts can be generalized. When skills are involved, this level would include more complicated skills involving numerous operations. At the level of values, you would relate facts and concepts to the life of the student. You would help the students explore the relationships between the subject and their feelings, opinions, and behavior.

SOCIAL STUDIES—GEORGE WASHINGTON
THE FATHER OF OUR COUNTRY

Purpose: To help intermediate-grade children learn more about George Washington by using a values approach.

Procedure: The students are asked to read about George Washington or are shown a film about his life. Some teachers may wish to tell or read a story that best illustrates the levels of facts, concepts, and values. The following questions are suggested at each level:

FACTS

1. Why is George Washington considered the Father of this country?
2. What happened when Washington was at Valley Forge?
3. What did George Washington do before the Revolutionary War?
4. Where did George Washington live before he became president?
5. Name two famous battles during the Revolutionary War.
6. What were the reasons why the colonies broke away from England?
7. Name four other leaders during the Revolutionary War.

CONCEPTS

1. What might have happened to George Washington if the British had won?
2. What qualities did George Washington have that made him a good leader?
3. What qualities do our present leaders have that are similar?
4. What qualities or events make a person a hero or a traitor?
5. How might the Revolutionary War have been prevented? What must be done to prevent wars?

VALUES

1. If you were at Valley Forge with George Washington what would you have done to stay alive? What is the most difficult situation you have had to face?
2. Pretend you are George Washington and write a letter to King George of England telling him how he could prevent the Revolutionary War.
3. What leadership roles have you had? How did you feel as a leader?
4. Were your ancestors living here during the Revolutionary War? What do you think they were doing? What would you have been doing if you were alive then?
5. If you had a chance to talk to George Washington, what questions would you want to ask him?
6. What would you do if foreign troops came to your house?

TEACHING COOPERATION THROUGH PHYSICAL EDUCATION IN JUNIOR HIGH SCHOOL

A majority of junior high school students are experiencing the onset of puberty, which can be a very difficult time for many of them. As their bodies are changing, so are many of their feelings, thoughts, attitudes, and behaviors. Socially, they are evolving from the more egocentric tendencies of the primary and intermediary grades and are becoming more interested in social relationships. Thus, it is an ideal time to foster the development of cooperation.

Because peer approval is important for junior high students and they are becoming interested in the opposite sex, they have a great need to prove themselves. This need, combined with their changing bodies and their resultant self-consciousness, can lead to inappropriate competition. Physical education can be designed to help students learn to interact cooperatively as they have fun and increase their physical coordination.

Purpose: To teach cooperation through physical education.

Procedure: The organization of these activities can be carried out by the teacher or shared by the students. Cooperation can be fostered by making it everyone's responsibility to decide and organize daily activities. As the teacher, your primary responsibility should be to act as an expert consultant who has certain skills many of your students may lack. The students' responsibilities are cooperatively to decide what games or sports they will play within the limitations of time, equipment, and environment, and to organize and carry these out.

A basic ground rule should be agreed upon by all members of the class: *There will be no losers; everyone can win.* This rule does not apply to the winning or losing of a game. Rather, it means that the group is interested in cooperation and in making sure that everyone gets what he or she wants out of the class a majority of the time. By allowing the students to decide and organize their activities cooperatively, this goal can be accomplished.

Assume this is the first day of a new physical education class. The following is a suggested procedure for implementing a cooperative organizational structure:

1. Explain that the choice and organization of activities will be shared by the students.
2. Provide the students with suggested games and sports and explain the limitations of time, equipment, and environment.
3. Explain your role—that you will help them learn rules or skills and that you will act as mediator if they have conflicts among them-

selves. Also, tell them any specific school rules or procedures they must follow.

4. Explain that because everyone is helping to decide and organize daily activities, everyone in the class should get to play desired games or sports much of the time. Also explain that a major reason for structuring the class in this way is to help them learn how to cooperate with each other. By cooperating, everyone can win; no one has to lose.

5. Ask them to agree to make sure that everyone in the class gets to play the games or sports he or she wants some of the time.

6. Ask if there are any questions. Does everyone understand what is going to happen in this class?

7. Suggest that you and they decide what activities you will do in the next week. Begin by asking for suggestions, for what they would like to play or learn. If there are some games or sports that they must learn, say so.

8. If there are a number of activities in which they are interested, you may want to suggest they organize them into units, or that they set up lists for each activity and sign up for what they would like to do on different days.

9. Ask them for ideas on how to organize activities: Who will take care of the equipment? How will teams be chosen? How will they use you if they need help?

10. Periodically, discuss how this plan is working. What problems are there? Is anyone not getting what he or she wants? How do they feel working together?

To the Teacher: Working together cooperatively is much more time-consuming at first than if you, as the teacher, decide what the students are going to do and when and how they will do it. You may feel impatient or frustrated as you try this method. However, if you perservere, you and your students will learn valuable skills in cooperation.

At first, you will probably want to take a fairly directive and active role in the process. Your task and your students' will be easier if you confront inappropriate competition, discounting, and/or passivity from the beginning. Fairly quickly, your students will be able to solve problems and cooperatively organize themselves with a minimum of guidance from you.

USING LEARNING CONTRACTS IN ENGLISH
LITERATURE IN HIGH SCHOOL

The use of learning contracts places the responsibility for learning on the student. It removes you as the teacher from the position of dictating what students will do and from the ensuing battle of wills that often results. Learning contracts also make clear what a student will do, how he or she will do it, and when the contract will be fulfilled. Because the contracts will be negotiated between you and your students, the students also gain the advantage of getting feedback about the acceptability of their plan before they carry it out.

Learning contracts are particularly appropriate in high school because students of this age can independently function quite effectively. If teachers and schools do not foster the opportunity for students to take responsibility for their own learning, they are likely to adopt a passive attitude, either compliant or rebellious. Learning contracts can help students think for themselves and decide what *they* want to learn.

Purpose: To teach *Hamlet* as part of a unit on Shakespeare by using learning contracts.

Procedures: To maximize the students' freedom and choice in what and how they will learn, allow them to choose what aspect of *Hamlet* they will explore. You may wish to give them some suggestions. To the extent that you are willing, also allow students to choose how they will present their learning, e.g., written essay, verbal report, art project, play, debate, etc.

After the class has read *Hamlet* and is ready to proceed with the projects, have students write out a rough draft of their learning contract. You may wish to use the sample form included here or devise one of your own. The contract should include the following:

1. today's date
2. student's name
3. what they will pursue in their learning project
4. how they will accomplish 3

5. how they will present it
6. what they will gain or learn or how they will benefit from doing it
7. how you and they will know if they accomplish their goal
8. what they want from you (for example, answers to specific questions)
9. when their project or essay will be completed
10. their signature and yours

When their rough contracts are completed, they should be discussed by you and each student and modified if necessary. You may also wish to have students contract for the grade they wish to receive. Be sure that the contracts are written in clear, concrete language.

When the contracts are complete, have students write them in final form. You and each student should have a copy. If students have difficulty meeting the terms of their contracts, they may renegotiate with you.

To the Teacher: Learning contracts can simplify your job because the primary responsibility for learning is placed on the student. Once students become accustomed to this approach, you will find that they are happier and that your class is an exciting experience for all of you.

Do not agree to any nonspecific, vague contracts, which are probably worse than no contract at all. They leave room for differences in interpretation and can cause hard feelings.

SAMPLE LEARNING CONTRACT

(today's date)

I, John Smith , will study/investigate Hamlet's self-revelation in *Hamlet* . I will accomplish this by studying *Hamlet* and at least three critical essays on the subject and present what I have learned by/in writing a 5- to 10-page paper . I will benefit or learn from this by gaining a better understanding of Shakespearean drama and having the experience of reading critical essays . You and I will know I have accomplished this by my being able to discuss my paper and the other

literary viewpoints with you ____. What I want from you is ____ for you to be
available to answer questions if I get stuck ____. I will complete this contract
by _____

      (date)

                                  _____

                                      (student's signature)

                                  _____

                                      (teacher's signature)

III

TRANSPERSONAL
SKILLS IN COMMUNICATION

ESSENTIAL TRANSPERSONAL
COMMUNICATION PROCESSES

The ability of a person to establish and maintain contact with his or her inner core is called transpersonal communication. At your core there is an awareness of your unity with all other people and a profound sense of connectedness with everything in your universe.

For most of us, reaching this core self means removing the barriers we have created to keep ourselves from experiencing our basic nature. The use of effective interpersonal and intrapersonal skills in communication is necessary if we are going to develop deeper and more basic transpersonal consciousness.

The concept of unity, or oneness, does not mean that everything is the same. Rather, it means that there is no real separation between us and our environment, including all the people in that environment. David Spangler put it simply: ". . . to communicate with a level of life apparently outside us, we simply discover and attune to its corresponding reality within us."[1] At the highest levels of transpersonal communication there ceases to be a reality within and a reality without.

Some of the essential transpersonal communication processes include centering, deep relaxation, concentration, energy awareness, imagery, peak experiences, unconditional love, dance, movement, and journal keeping. This section will describe each of these processes and provide activities to help you learn to communicate at deeper levels with yourself and others.

Transpersonal communication seeks to provide a framework for the development of direct intuitive knowing and being. In teaching these skills to your students you will need to

1. model the skills; demonstrate your own willingness to trust your intuitive knowledge
2. create an accepting atmosphere that nurtures and supports the discovery of internal and subjective sources of knowledge and being
3. provide learning activities that focus on the development of these processes and skills
4. allow your students to design some of their own learning activities and take turns leading the ones you design

[1]David Spangler, in eds. Dolores LaChapelle and Janet Bourque, *Earth Festivals*, (Silverton, Col.: Finn Hill Arts Publishers, 1974).

13

Below
Your Navel

BACK TO BASICS: TEACHING PEOPLE HOW
TO SIT, STAND, WALK, AND BREATHE

Recently in America there has been a swing back to a no-frills type of education which emphasizes reading, writing, and arithmetic. This change was prompted by reports of high school graduates who were functionally illiterate.

Unfortunately, what is being proposed seems like an inadequate solution to a problem we are only beginning to understand. When this solution fails like so many have before, we will again be left wondering where we went wrong. It is true that we have neglected basics, but not the basics we are currently focusing upon. In a transpersonal sense, there are basics we have only begun to bring to awareness, and the truth about our unity with the universe has to be experienced at an everyday level. George Leonard put it this way: "Transformation begins with the way you stand, walk and breathe."[1] He suggests that we should spend the first several

[1]George Leonard, *The Transformation* (New York: Dell Publishing Co., 1972), p. 224.

years of school teaching children how to sit, stand, walk, and breathe, and if we did, the way children learn would be truly transformed.[2]

We know that we realize so little of our potential (estimates range from 3 to 8 percent), and yet we still do not know how to enable people to learn and grow in ways we can only begin to imagine. Transpersonal communication emphasizes that the search lies in a broader understanding of human functioning. In the Castenada books, we begin to get a glimpse of the separate reality that has eluded our grasp. According to Don Juan, there are two basic ways of perceiving reality. One he calls "looking," which is simply perceiving the world in its usually accepted forms. The other way, which he believes is attained only after years of disciplined effort, he calls "seeing."

It is at times obvious to some of us that this separate reality is real and is tantalizingly close by. It may take only one small step over an invisible line to reach a place where everything flows in universal harmony. It is our suspicion that children are probably closer to that reality than most adults. Joseph Chilton Pearce, in a mind-opening book called *The Magical Child*,[3] documents what he calls nature's plan for children. According to Pearce, the basic altered state of consciousness, or separate reality, if you wish, is the playful state of a child. He says that child's play, which we often label as nonproductive and even antisurvival, is the key that unlocks the door to the separate reality. Our children have been crying out to us for years, telling us that things are critically wrong with them, and for the most part we have been deaf and blind to their calls of distress.

There is indeed danger in trying to teach anything in school. The standard joke is that the way to get teenagers disinterested in sex is by teaching it in school. Since we have made the commitment to having schools and to teaching certain skills and information, we must make a decision about what to teach.

What we are suggesting in this book is that you as a teacher or counselor begin to bring a new focus, a transpersonal focus, to children in your school. If your school is emphasizing basics, then extend those basics to include the ones described in this book. Help children learn to breathe, sit, stand, and walk in new ways that enable them to learn in new ways the

---

[2]George Leonard, statement made at a conference, Kansas City, Missouri, October 1974.

[3]Joseph Chilton Pearce, *The Magical Child* (New York: E. P. Dutton, 1977).

other important basic skills of reading, writing, and arithmetic. If you are teaching in upper grades or junior or senior high school, these exercises are equally valuable. They can be incorporated into any teaching in the classroom or used separately as a warm-up or settling-down activity to provide needed transitions during the school day.

CENTERING

Where is your center? Take a minute and think about where you center your being. Is it in your head? Is it in your heart? Is it in your lower abdomen? In fact, it is in all those places. Your mind may serve as your intellectual center, your heart may be the center of your emotions, and your lower abdomen may serve as the physical balancing center of your body. The experience of being *centered* involves an integration or balance among all these forces. It is the inner feeling of well-being, calmness, and strength you can feel in any activity you do.

Many people have lost a sense of where their physical center is located. We may spend so much time thinking and emphasizing intellectual activities in school that children may believe their physical center to be in their heads. In any case, this overemphasis can make us raise our natural center of gravity, which is usually about two inches below the navel. We tend to let our energy go up and out of our body instead of down and in, and as a result, tend to get "ahead of ourselves."

You can sit, stand, walk, play baseball, make love, or read a book from a centered place or an uncentered place. If you are feeling anxious or tense or are preoccupied by thoughts of the past or future, it is difficult to stay centered. Learning to notice the difference is an important awareness, as is learning how to return to center when it is necessary.

The goal of centering is not to learn how to stay centered all the time, for that would be impossible. The goal instead is to know when you are centered and when you are not. Only when you have that awareness can you return to center when you notice you have been pulled away by some thought, feeling, or action. Health and well-being can be defined as the amount of time it takes you to return to center; the shorter the time the healthier you are.

HOW TO TEACH CENTERING AWARENESS

ACTIVITY 30—CENTERING BREATH

Rationale: This activity is designed to help you focus your energy down and into your natural center of gravity by using breathing. Many people have learned to breathe backward, holding their stomach in and pushing their chest out as they inhale. They may have trouble at first expanding their abdomen as they inhale and letting it fall naturally when they exhale.

Step 1: Ask the children to stand so they can swing their arms from side to side without touching anyone. Ask them to swing their arms gently from side to side, wrapping them around their bodies. Their feet should be spread at shoulder width and their knees bent slightly. Shoulders and arms should be relaxed. Let them do this exercise for one minute.

Step 2: Ask them to stand still, with their eyes closed and breathing in through their noses and out through their mouths. Have them breathe into their abdomen so that it rises with each incoming breath and falls with each exhaling one. Have them do this step for four or five breaths.

Step 3: Now have them press firmly with their right index fingers on a point about two inches below the navel. After one minute have them drop their hands and continue to imagine breathing to and from that spot. Say, "Allow the air to enter through your nostrils and travel downward to that spot. Fill your abdomen with your incoming breath, and as you exhale bring the air upward from that spot." Have them continue this breathing for several minutes.

Step 4: A variation of this activity is to ask them to breathe only into their upper chest and then change back to breathing into their center. Discuss the differences they may have noticed.

To the Teacher: This is a beginning exercise to help children build awareness of breathing to and from their centers. After initial instruction, some regular practice is helpful. It is advisable to use this activity before introducing any new learning or an activity that might produce anxiety in some children. Simply say, "Let's do five or six centering breaths before we start this."

To help children learn the connection between being centered and their ability to do well in various activities, discuss with them some of the following questions: "What happens to your breathing when you get scared or angry?" "Why do some people seem to think better when they are breathing into their center?" "What are some other advantages to breathing into your center?" "What are some ways you can tell when you are uncentered?" "What are some ways you use to get uncentered? Centered?"

ACTIVITY 31—CHANGING YOUR CENTER

Rationale: This activity demonstrates dramatically how you can change your center of gravity and energy flow just by thinking. It should not be used with anyone who has a serious back problem.

Step 1: Have class members select partners who are about their same weight and height. Taking turns, have one class member stand the way the child would normally while the other class member lifts him or her by wrapping his or her arms around the partner's waist from behind. Ask them to notice how much energy it took to lift their partners.

Step 2: Now ask the same child to become centered by using breathing. Then ask the class members to imagine that they are sending their energy down through their legs and out the bottom of their feet. Ask them to imagine that their energy is going into the ground and spreading out like roots, keeping them firmly planted on the ground. Instruct them to focus all their thoughts on moving their energy downward in their bodies and out the bottoms of their feet while they continue to breathe into their center.

Step 3: When they indicate they are ready (when their energy is focused downward), they should signal to their partners to lift them as before. Partners should be cautioned not to lift suddenly but to make a slow, gradual lift. Ask them to notice any differences in the amount of energy required to lift their partners.

Step 4: Now, ask them to reverse the energy and send it upward through their bodies and out the tops of their heads. They should think of their bodies becoming light as a feather. When they are ready they should signal their partners to lift them as before and notice the difference. Have the partners reverse roles so both can have the experience.

Variation: Some students may believe that the power of suggestion was a factor, so have them do this exercise with the students not telling their partners which way they are sending their energy.

To the Teacher: If done correctly, your students should have an awareness of significant differences during the three conditions. They may not understand why they have occurred, and some discussion is desirable. Ask them what they think accounted for the differences. Also, discuss the application of this skill to sports, classroom activities, and activities at home. "When is it good to lower your center and when is it good to raise it?"

This activity also shows clearly that your students can learn to develop conscious control over their centeredness. For many students the awareness of their own power is quite comforting and can lead them to assume more internal control of their lives and well-being.

ACTIVITY 32—STANDING AND WALKING
FROM YOUR CENTER

Rationale: Any movement such as standing, walking, running, bending, or stretching involves a flow of motion. However, most of us have lost contact with that flow. If you watch people walk you can see many different styles. Some people walk firmly and deliberately, others very hesitantly. Some walk with their hands way out in front of themselves, and they are likely to be "ahead of themselves" in most things they do and say. Learning to walk from the center involves a higher level of awareness of your movements and how they flow in harmony with your being and your environment.

Step 1: This activity can take place in the classroom, on the playground or school grounds, or in a natural setting away from school. The first step is to get your students to stand from the center. Ask them to use the centering breath throughout this activity. In addition, first have them stand as they would usually.

Step 2: Now begin a progressive centering by using the following instructions: "Start by getting your feet centered under your body. Roll on the outside and inside of your feet to feel the limits, and then your toes and heels, until you find that spot where your feet feel centered under your body. Now center your knees over your feet. Keep them bent slightly and relaxed. Now locate the place where your trunk and pelvis are centered over your knees and feet. Move from side to side and front to back until you find that comfortable centered spot. Now move your upper trunk and spine so that it feels centered over your pelvis. Again experiment with various positions until you find one that feels centered and comfortable. Next, set your shoulders in a comfortable, centered position on top of your trunk. Move them around and keep them relaxed. Finally, place your neck and head in a centered position on top of your body. Now go back down through your body to your feet and back again to the top of your head, checking out your centeredness. Stay relaxed and breathe fully into your physical center."

Step 3: Say to the class, "Now you are ready to practice walking from center. As you walk, pay close attention to each movement you make. Keep your eyes open and focus on the ground about six feet ahead of you. Keep your head erect with your eyes focused slightly downward. Walk at a moderately slow pace, with steps small enough, without losing your balance, to lift one foot and place it firmly on the ground before moving the next foot. [Demonstrate this walk several times for your students before they start.] Remember to pay attention to the flow of the movement *as it occurs*."

Step 4: Then say, "To help us quiet our minds during this activity say the following sentence first aloud with me and then silently to yourself as you walk: 'I hear, I see, and I feel the flow.' Now say it again aloud with me: 'I hear, I see, and I feel the flow.' Good. . . . When you are ready start walking. Be careful not to bump into anyone or anything. Be totally aware of where you are and what you are doing. We will do this for the next _____ minutes and I will ring this tiny bell when we are finished. Are there any questions?"

To the Teacher: This activity involves a different kind of learning for many students. Follow the activity with a discussion about what they learned. One way to structure the discussion is by asking them to respond to a series of open-ended statements like "I learned that . . . ," "I was surprised that . . . ," "I discovered that . . . ," etc.

RELAXATION

Another basic transpersonal process is to learn how to relax and let go of any tensions you might carry in your body. Most of us carry chronic levels of tension, which we have come to accept as a normal way of functioning. There are obvious benefits to relaxation training in helping students score better on tests, do better in various sports, and develop social skills. Below are some relaxation training exercises you can use with yourself and your students when you are feeling tense.

ACTIVITY 33—RELAXATION BREATHING

Retionale: Sometimes you may need a quick, effective method of relaxation when you find yourself getting tense in the middle of an activity.

Step 1: When you inhale say to yourself, "I am." When you exhale say to yourself, "relaxed." Thus the complete cycle is inhale (I am) and exhale (relaxed). Breathe fully and completely but don't exaggerate your breath or hold it before or after exhaling.

Step 2: Do this activity as often and as long as you need it.

To the Teacher: You can use this exercise routinely with your class before each new activity or if you sense some tension in your students. Some teachers place this activity on a poster on the wall to remind students to use it when they need it.

ACTIVITY 34—CLEANSING BREATH

Rationale: Just as in Activity 33, you can extend the relaxation training by using only breathing. This activity uses breathing to free the mind and body of any tension.

Step 1: Ask your students to lie on their backs (or to be seated) with their eyes closed and to breathe in through their noses and out through their mouths.

Step 2: Give your students the following instructions: "Close your eyes, breathe deeply and fully, in through your nose and out through your mouth. Do not force or strain your breath. Do this for several minutes to develop a breathing rhythm."

Step 3: Tell your students, "Now as you breathe in, concentrate on breathing *light* into your body, and as you exhale concentrate on breathing out *toxins*. Do this for five or six breaths."

Step 4: Tell them, "Now as you inhale, concentrate on breathing in *strength*, and as you exhale breathe out *tension*. Do this for five or six breaths."

Step 5: Then say, "As you inhale, concentrate on breathing in *love*, and as you exhale focus on breathing out *fear*. Continue this breathing until you feel your body is completely relaxed. If you find tension in any part of your body, breathe love into that part and release the tension when you exhale. Fill your whole body with light, strength, and love. When you feel ready, open your eyes slowly and sit quietly and calmly."

To the Teacher: This is an important skill, and like any other, it takes practice for your students to get full benefit from it. You can use it with those students who seem to have chronic tension or "dis-ease" in their body. Students with learning disabilities can also profit greatly from the cleansing effects of this activity.

CONCENTRATION

One of the most important skills in the learning process is concentration, or the ability to focus attention on any one thing for a duration of time. In addition to being an important learning skill, training in concentration is an essential transpersonal communication. The ability to be deeply aware of what you are doing and not to be distracted is difficult to learn. A student who has developed a high level of concentration usually can condense bodies of facts and information in such a way that the deeper and more synthesized meaning becomes readily apparent. Training in concentration leads to a centered calmness, where you can focus your attention completely on a task or problem and detach yourself from internal and external distractions. Although this training often takes years, children can begin to profit from it quite quickly.

ACTIVITY 35—SITTING

Rationale: It would be simple if we could just "decide" to concentrate. However, we are conditioned to not concentrate, or focus our minds, but to be aware of many things at the same time. Thus we have to retrain our minds in the practice of concentration. One such activity is simply called "sitting."

Step 1: Have your students sit in a comfortable position with their eyes closed and backs straight but not rigid.

Step 2: Ask them to place their complete attention on the rising and falling of their abdomens as they breathe. They do not have to say the words, "rising and falling"; they must just focus their attention on the actual process of their abdomens rising during an incoming breath and falling during an outgoing one. Ask them to breathe normally; and if their minds drift off on thoughts, feelings, or other sensations, they should simply be aware of them and then calmly return to focusing on the rising and falling of their abdomens.

Step 3: Tell your students to develop awareness in noticing any thoughts, feelings, or sensations as they occur and then to return quickly to their primary focus. The quicker they notice, the quicker they can let go of any thoughts.

Step 4: Daydreaming will occur, and the students' minds will wander. Instruct them not to judge themselves, but simply to note that they were daydreaming; then they should refocus on their breathing.

To the Teacher: This may seem like an idle exercise, but the results can be truly startling. At first, you and your students may find it difficult to stay focused for more than several seconds at a time. With practice you can gradually increase the time. One minute of pure concentration is a fairly high objective for beginners, so don't set your sights too high. Start "sitting" for short periods of time: one to three minutes for elementary students, and five to six minutes for secondary students. Gradually build it up to longer periods if your schedule permits. This is an excellent activity to start the school day, provided there is a time free from interruptions.

The content or focus of the concentration is not as important as the process. You can have the children count their breaths, focus on a single sound, look at a geometric design, such as a triangle, or visualize an object in their minds. Explain to students that this training will help them make friends with their own minds and thoughts as well as help them learn more easily. Questions you might use to stimulate discussion are as follows: What is concentration? Give definitions and examples. What are some other ways to concentrate that have worked for you? What are some additional ways you would like to try? What are some benefits of practicing concentration (in school, at play, at home, etc.)?

ACTIVITY 36—VISUAL CONCENTRATION

Rationale: This form of training enables you to expand your frame of reference while focusing on a single object, like a candle.

Step 1: Have everyone gather around a single candle, or if you have a large group, divide into several small groups (ten to twelve in a group), each with its own candle. Turn out the lights and close the blinds so the only illumination is coming from the candle. Your students can sit on the floor or stay seated at their desks if they are movable.

Step 2: Ask your students to bring all their attention to looking deep inside the flame of the candle. After everyone has focused his or her attention for several minutes, move to the next step.

Step 3: Say, "Now move your attention inside the flame of the candle so you feel as if you're sitting inside of it and become one with it [pause about one minute]. If you are getting distracted just be aware of that happening and return to focusing attention on the candle flame."

Step 4: Tell them, "Now imagine the whole group sitting inside the candle flame with you [pause about one minute]."

Step 5: Say to the class, "Now come out of the candle flame and say good-bye to it."

To the Teacher: The outcome of this activity is not easy to predict. You may want to have your students write about the experience or draw a picture that illustrates it. If you discuss it, ask questions like the following: "What did you learn about yourself in doing this activity?" "What did you find distracted you the most while you were concentrating?" "How did you feel being inside the candle flame?" "How did you feel having the group there with you?"

14

High Energy: Activities in Energy Awareness for the Classroom

ENERGY AWARENESS

A field of energy exists in and around each of us. This subtle energy moves through our bodies, pulsating in waves. Sometimes we feel low in energy and sometimes we are filled with high energy. What causes the difference? No one is totally sure but some interesting hypotheses currently are being tested. One such hypothesis suggests that our thoughts are energy, and the quality of those thoughts determines the level and quality of the energy in our bodies. Another hypothesis suggests that the more we relax and center our bodies, the more energy we will have.

A number of martial arts from Far Eastern cultures have been studying and using principles of energy awareness for many centuries. Two of these deserve mention. One is Tai Chi, a Chinese martial art, which involves learning precise movements to connect with what is called "chi" energy. This connection enables the individual to operate in harmony and balance with the laws of the universe. Aikido, a Japanese martial art of more modern origin, makes use of a similar concept called "ki." The founder, Morihei Uyeshiba wrote, "The secret of aikido is to harmonize ourselves with the movement of the universe and bring ourselves into accord with the universe itself. He who has gained the secret of aikido has the universe in himself and can say, 'I am the universe.' "[1]

The harmonizing of personal and universal energy is essential to the deep awareness of unity and connectedness which is your basic nature. For the most part, all of us have lost touch with this connection. We have chosen to forget who we are, and we have forgotten that we chose to forget. Activities in energy awareness are one way you can begin to re-experience your basic core self.

For many people, their basic experience with themselves and others is one of paranoia or a deep sense of isolation and separation. The opposite experience, which most of us have had only momentarily, is *harmonia*, or a sense of deep connection with self and others. This harmony exists all around you and is waiting there to be experienced. Energy awareness builds upon the skills of centering, breathing, relaxation, and concentration presented in the previous chapter.

The purpose of the activities in this chapter is to help you and your students experience this energy and begin to learn how to use this awareness to reconnect with your core self and with universal energy. Another important objective is to enable you and your students to begin to experience the amount of conscious control you can have over your energy and well-being.

ACTIVITY 37—TURNING ON OUR OWN ENERGY

Rationale: This activity will enable you and your students actually to feel the subtle energy that flows through your body. Through a process of "turning up the volume" on this energy, you can begin to understand its properties and experience the flow.

Step 1: Have your students stand and do centering breathing for a short period. Have them take off their shoes and any jewelry and loosen their belts.

Step 2: Have your students press and spread the fingers of one hand against the other hand at the the fingertips. Have them hold their palms down with the heels of their hands as much apart as possible.

Step 3: Now, maintaining the fingertip contact, have them turn their

[1]George Leonard, *The Ultimate Athlete* (New York: Avon Books, 1977), p. 63.

fingertips inward, pointing toward their chests. Ask them to hold this position while maintaining the pressure on the fingers for one minute while breathing naturally.

Step 4: Then ask them to break the contact, shake their hands vigorously for about ten to twenty seconds, and then let their hands relax at their sides.

Step 5: Ask them to close their eyes and experience the sensations in their arms and hands.

Step 6: Ask them to place their hands about six inches apart, with their palms facing each other, and make contact with their own energy. Ask them to move their hands further apart and closer together to sense the differences.

To the Teacher: Ask the students how they would describe the sensations they felt in their arms and hands, to say just a word or two describing the sensation of feeling. Write all the words on the board, indicating that there is no right or wrong way to feel. Also ask if there was anyone who didn't feel anything. If anyone had that experience, reassure him or her that this is a skill and may take time to develop. Tell the students in the meantime to act as if they had felt something, seeing if later on they actually do begin to feel sensations. Discuss the fact that we may not have adequate words to describe fully this energy, and ask the students to invent new words that are descriptive of what they experienced. They may come up with words like "wooshy," "zippy," or "dynoripple."

Another way to increase awareness of energy is to ask the students to act out or do a pantomime of what energy means to them.

ACTIVITY 38—SHARING ENERGY

Rationale: Once you have made contact with your own energy, the next step is to begin to learn how to share energy with others. This activity should follow the first one, either immediately or at another time.

Step 1: Ask your students to select a partner to work with them on this activity. Do the hand-excitation exercise described in Activity 37, or ask them to shake their hands vigorously.

Step 2: Ask them to stand facing their partners, make eye contact, and without speaking lift their hands with palms facing their partners' palms. Have them move so their palms are about six inches apart. Then ask them to relax their bodies and breathe to and from their centers.

Step 3: Ask them to feel the sensations coming from their partners in the palms and fingers of their hands.

Step 4: Have them move their hands up and down or from side to side slightly to feel the contact move with them. Have them move back from their partners and feel the differences.

Step 5: If they start to lose the contact or have trouble establishing it, ask them to shake their hands vigorously for about thirty seconds and then try again. Also, be sure to remind them to keep their shoulders relaxed.

Variation: If you have room to allow the students to move around, you can extend this activity. Ask them to walk around the room backward, sideways, and forward, alternating these instructions. Occasionally ask them to stop, get themselves centered, and see if they can restore contact with their partners. After you have done this step for several minutes, ask them to move slowly with their eyes closed; then have them stop, and without opening their eyes, again make contact with their partners' energy.

To the Teacher: This activity and its variation may give your students a solid experience in making contact with others and can be followed by a variety of similar activities. Plants and even inanimate objects such as rocks give off energy vibrations. If you have plants in your room, have your students regularly exchange energy with them, always remembering to send loving thoughts and energy to the plants. You may begin to notice some highly unusual changes in your plants. An interesting experiment would be to pay specific attention to some plants and not to others, noticing what differences in rates of growth occur.

Pyramid power, or focusing energy by using the geometric shape of the pyramid, can also help your students understand the natural energy forces in the universe. Placing plants or other objects under a pyramid and comparing them with identical objects not so placed clearly shows some startling effects. A good resource on pyramid power is *The Psychic Power of Pyramids*.[2]

[2]Bill Schul and Ed Pettit, *The Psychic Power of Pyramids* (Greenwich, Conn.: Fawcett Publications, Inc., 1976).

ACTIVITY 39—THOUGHT ENERGY

Rationale: Our thoughts are a source of energy and a directing force. When we have loving and positive thoughts toward ourselves and others, we can become open channels for our energy to flow through and we can freely give and receive positive energy to and from others. Students with poor self-images generally repeat negative thoughts about themselves and others and have closed down their energy flow.

Step 1: Ask your students to write the following sentence: "I am loved just for being alive." They then write any negative thoughts that occur to them immediately after writing the positive sentence (e.g., "I have to do something to get people to love me.")

Step 2: Have them change each of the negative thoughts into a positive thought and write that down in another sentence (e.g., "People love me even when I am not doing anything.")

Step 3: Have them repeat this process until they can write positive statements about themselves without any negative thoughts occurring to deny the positive energy.

To the Teacher: This is an important activity to help build a positive self-image in yourself and your students. It is recommended that you use it every day at first to help strengthen positive thinking and remove any blocks. Write other appropriate messages on the board, and help each student learn to use this process.

Another important use of this activity is to prepare students for specific academic experiences. For example, before starting a math class ask the students to write a sentence such as the following: "I am open and receptive to learning mathematics." Then ask them to notice any negative thoughts that come up (e.g., "He may expect too much" or "He may not like me if I don't understand"). Encourage students to ask for what they want or need in order to be successful at learning math.

ACTIVITY 40—SENDING LOVING ENERGY

Rationale: Positive or loving energy is like a wave that goes from one person to another. This activity can help you and your students experience the good feelings that come from sending and receiving loving energy to each other.

Step 1: Have everyone sit in a circle facing each other. Ask each person to tell the group three things that he or she likes about himself or herself.

Step 2: After one person shares three things, then the group members are asked to tell that person at least six things they like about him or her that were not mentioned by the person. Be aware that these remarks should be totally positive, with no qualifiers. Also watch for nonverbal signs that those receiving the positive energy are deflecting it instead of letting it in, for example, breaking eye contact, smiling nervously, shrugging the shoulders.

Step 3: Take turns until everyone, including you, has had an opportunity to complete the activity.

Step 4: After everyone has finished, have the students join hands and close their eyes. Ask them to picture each student in the group and send loving thoughts to them one by one.

Step 5: Ask them to open their eyes and make eye contact with each person in the group.

To the Teacher: This is a powerful activity, so time should be provided at the end for discussion. Ask questions like the following: "How did you feel saying positive things about yourself in the group?" "How did you feel receiving positive messages from your classmates?" "What are some ways you used to block the positive energy?"

A variation of this activity is to have your students send loving, positive thoughts to those people they think don't like them or to those people they don't like. This step may draw the other person to them, or at least they will feel satisfied that they have done their best in giving.

ACTIVITY 41—PROTECTING YOUR ENERGY

Rationale: There are people who try to steal energy from others when they themselves feel low because often they don't know how to regenerate their own energy. Actually, no one can steal energy from you unless you let him. The purposes of this activity are (1) to help you become more aware of the ways you allow others to steal your energy, and (2) to help you learn some ways to protect your energy. Most successful teachers and counselors have to learn how to protect their energy or they quickly will become victims of "burn out." It is easy to get pulled off center by energy snatchers, but the goal is not to always remain centered. Rather, a good definition of emotional health is *how quickly you can return to center after being pulled off* by an event or situation.

Step 1: Ask your students to select a partner to work with whom they know and trust. Ask them to sit facing each other in a place in the room where they won't interfere with others.

Step 2: Ask them during this activity to use all the centering, relaxation, and concentration techniques they have learned to help them protect their energy.

Step 3: Taking turns, one member starts by telling his or her partner about a recent decision that he or she feels good about. It can be a decision to buy something or to go somewhere or to do something— whatever he or she feels free to share. Limit the telling to several minutes.

Step 4: After one member of the pair has shared her or his story, the other member is instructed to try to talk him or her out of the decision. In other words, the other person will try to steal energy by disparaging the decision of his or her partner.

Step 5: The person who shared the decision is merely to sit and listen to the attack without responding verbally. Ask the students instead to pay attention to the thoughts, feelings, and sensations they have while their partners try to steal energy. These become important clues to possible weak spots where that person may be most vulnerable to energy snatching.

Step 6: After one member of the pair has completed the activity, then the roles are reversed.

To the Teacher: The discussion that follows this activity is very important. Some questions you might consider asking are as follows: "What thoughts, feelings, and sensations in your body were you aware of while your decision was being attacked?" "What are some of the most common ways that people let others steal energy from them?" (Make a list on the board, which may include such things as "not breathing fully," "trying to defend your decision," "needing to be right," "feeling put down person-ally by what others say," "putting others down," etc.) "In what situations do you find it hard or easy to protect your energy?" "During this activity what did you find worked best for you in protecting your energy?" (Make a list on the board, which may include, "I used the centering breath," "I repeated a calming message to myself like 'I am relaxed.' ") "What are some of the early warning signals to help you identify energy snatchers?" (Again make a list on the board that grows out of the discussion. It might include characteristics, such as "people who have a 'whine' in their voice," or critical or judgmental statements, "people with negative at-titudes about self and others"; etc.)

ACTIVITY 42—GENERATING HIGH ENERGY IN GROUPS

Rationale: Some people who steal energy don't realize what they are doing and don't know other ways to generate energy for themselves. Many of the centering, relaxation, and concentration activities can be used to generate energy for yourself when you need it. In addition, the following group activity shows how energy can be shared so that all in-volved receive higher levels.

Step 1: Have all your students sit in a circle holding hands.

Step 2: Taking turns, have everybody send loving energy to each per-son, one at a time. Say something like, "Now everyone close your eyes and send loving energy from your core to [name of student]." Transmit the energy consciously but nonverbally until each student has the direct experience of receiving it at a core level.

To the Teacher: By the time each student has had a turn, there is usually a build-up of loving energy in the circle and in the whole room which is easily recognizable by each person. The whole group now may be aware of the energy they have channeled and created, and they may feel bathed in new energy. Following this energy boost, you will find the students peaceful, calm, and open and receptive to learning new skills.

A variation of this activity is to have the group send loving energy to someone from the class who is absent or to anyone that a student suggests is in need of it.

ACTIVITY 43—ALL IS ENERGY

Rationale: This activity is designed to help you go beyond the usual dimensions of energy awareness and experience yourself as pure energy outside the confines of your body. This is an advanced activity and should be used only after some of the other activities in this chapter.

Step 1: Ask your students to lie on their backs on the floor (or to be seated if necessary). Darken the room as much as possible and have them close their eyes. Use the following instructions:

Step 2: "Be very still and quiet, making sure you are comfortable and not touching your neighbor. Feel your toes; (pause) now feel them disappear into light. (pause) Now feel your feet; (pause) feel them disappear into light. (pause) See only light in your mind's eye where your feet once were."

Step 3: "Now feel your ankles and see them disappear into light. (pause) Feel your legs and feel them disappear into light."

Step 4: "Feel your trunk and pelvis and visualize them slowly disappearing and becoming pure white light."

Step 5: "Now feel your upper body, your stomach, chest, back, and shoulders and feel them all slowly disappearing and becoming pure light. (pause) Now feel your arms disappearing into light."

Step 6: "Now concentrate on your neck and head; your chin, mouth, nose, eyes, ears, and hair are disappearing into a beam of pure white light. (pause) Your whole head is disappearing into light."

Step 7: "Recheck in your mind where your body previously was located and see if there are any parts that have not disappeared completely. (pause) If they haven't, feel them disappear now."

Step 8: "Now you have no body. It has entirely disappeared into light. Go deep inside the core of you, that part of you that is beyond your body. Feel that core filled with loving, radiant energy."

Step 9: "Now starting with your head, bring your body back from the light. This time as each part reappears it is filled with loving, radiant energy. Now your upper body . . . your trunk . . . your arms . . . your legs . . . your ankles, feet, and toes. When you are ready, open your eyes feeling calm, rested, and full of pure energy."

To the Teacher: This can be a powerful transpersonal experience for you and your students, so some discussion may be necessary to help them integrate it into their ordinary reality. You may ask, "What did you experience during this activity?" "What parts of your body did you have the hardest time letting disappear?" "What are some reasons why you were reluctant to let go?"

15

It's Only Your Imagination

IMAGINATION

Our imagination, or ability to make the images of our lives, serves as the wellspring of all our hopes and fears. Our hopes and fears help create our recurring attitudes and thoughts, which we use in turn to create the world around us and everything that happens to us, which in turn help re-create our emotions and images in a never-ending sequence.

When we become fully aware that we are willfully creating our reality out of our imagination all the time, we can become fully alive to the limitless power of the creative mind. To be without imagination is to be dead. In this chapter we will explore more fully the use of training in imagination as a vital transpersonal communication process.

THE REPRESENTATIONAL WORLD

When we talk to one another about our experiences we are not telling each other about how those experiences *actually happened*. What we do is represent that experience as we perceive it, not as it actually happened.

(This concept was discussed in Chapter 2 on external awareness.) We know that these perceptions do form the basis for our communication with each other. Each of us has his or her own favorite way of organizing his or her perceptions. Some people are visual people, which means that they tend to look at experiences, develop a picture or image of that experience, and then represent the experience to others by using a highly visual language. They may say "I *saw* this man talking to several other people" or "I *looked* for my keys in my purse" or "I *see* what you mean." By listening to the verbs and predicates they use most often, you can begin to identify the form of thinking they like best. An auditory person might say "I *heard* this man talking to several other people" or "I *hear* what you are saying;" and a kinesthetic person would "get a *feel* for the person" or say "I *felt* for my keys in my purse." This perception may be interesting and startling to you if you haven't been aware of the way you or others represent experiences. In addition, it is vital to the understanding of how people learn. For example, if you discover someone's favorite representational system and you use the same system in responding to that person, he or she will understand you far easier than if you use a different representational system. If someone were telling you about an experience and said, "I *heard* this man talking to several other people," and you were to ask, "What did he *look* like?"—he or she may not even understand why it is important for you to know the answer. Considerable miscommunication probably occurs as a result of two people using different representational systems.

Some people learn better from reading, others from hearing, and still others from touching. The best educational process would be one that uses all three forms, enabling students to expand their perceptual base. In this chapter, we will try to use all three representational systems in the activities we discuss. Instead of thinking about just visual aids, you may need to include auditory and kinesthetic ones as well.

TRAINING IN IMAGINATION

ACTIVITY 44—THE WATERFALL OF LIGHT

Rationale: This activity is designed to develop a sensory awareness of life energy, to create a sense of unity of mind, body, and spirit. Notice that the instructions encourage visual, auditory, and kinesthetic imagining.

Step 1: Ask your students to sit comfortably with their eyes closed, either in their chairs or on the floor. Give them the following instructions:

Step 2: "Imagine a waterfall of white light located about three inches above your head and feel it flowing into the top of your head and through your whole body. If you listen closely you can hear the water coming into your body, see it becoming a stream of white light, and feel it flowing down throughout your body."

Step 3: "Feel the water pouring over your face and into your neck. Picture the stream of water–light pouring into every corner and crevice of your body. Now feel it filling up your arms and gushing into your chest and heart. Listen to it rush down into your stomach. What sound is the light making as it moves down through your body?"

Step 4: "Feel the water making its way down through your legs and feet until your whole body is part of the waterfall of light."

Step 5: "See this light whirling through your body, seeking out dark corners where the water has not yet reached. Feel those areas opening up and hear the water rushing in, filling that area with white light."

Step 6: "Feel yourself becoming this white light. The white light is you and you are the white light."

Step 7: "You are now a whirling waterfall of white light and you can go anywhere and do anything you want to do. Take some time now to imagine doing something or going somewhere as a whirling white light." (Pause three to six minutes.)

Step 8: "Now come back to this room, slowly open your eyes, and be prepared to share what you did and where you went."

To the Teacher: Instead of verbal sharing, you can ask the students to write about their experience or draw pictures representing it.

ACTIVITY 45—THE WHEEL OF IMAGINATION

Rationale: This activity involves the creation and use of group imagination. Very often the imaginative stirrings of one person can stimulate the imagination of another. This activity provides a structure for unlimited imaginings.

Step 1: Divide the larger group into subgroups of six to eight students each. Have the members of each small group lie on their backs with their feet together, touching each others' feet in the center of the circle. Where their feet are touching is the hub of the wheel. Their heads form part of the rim, and the rest of their bodies form the spokes.

Step 2: Have them close their eyes and join hands with the person on each side. Use the following instructions: "Imagine yourself moving; imagine the whole wheel moving around and around to the left. (pause–30 seconds) Now feel it moving the other way, around and around to the right. Feel it moving as the heart of the whole universe. Your wheel is the heart of the universe. As a part of this wheel you are a part of everything, everyone, everywhere. See your wheel moving through space and time. (pause) Hear the sounds of the universe blending with you as you travel."

Step 3: When someone feels like taking the wheel somewhere or doing something in the universe he or she can begin by saying, "I am the wheel of imagination and I am taking all of you with me to [a place or thing]." That person continues to describe where they are going and what they see, hear, and feel when they get there.

Step 4: Tell the other students to add, change, expand, or contract the images at any time. Ask questions like "What do you see there?" "What sounds are you aware of?" "What does that feel like?" "When you touch that object what is it like?"

Step 5: Continue the imaginary trips and scenes as long as the group is involved in the activity. If one image is bogging down, suggest that someone else take over the wheel of imagination.

To the Teacher: This activity can be used as part of academic subjects. You might want to use it to extend the learning in a particular unit or to introduce new content.

ACTIVITY 46—MY SECRET HIDING PLACE

Rationale: This activity is designed to use the imagination to open up awareness of inner space and provide an imaginary place where people can retreat to when they are scared, confused, or low in energy. This activity can help them develop an inner sanctuary.

Step 1: Ask the children to remain seated and to close their eyes. Use the following instructions: "Imagine that you are becoming small, so small that you can go inside your body. (pause) Decide how you are going to get inside your body. (pause) Now do it. (pause) Explore what it is like to be inside your body. (pause) Look all around your body. (pause) What colors do you see? (pause) What sounds do you hear coming from inside your body? How does it feel being inside? Do you feel crowded or is there lots of space?"

Step 2: Say, "Now look around for hiding places inside your body. (pause) Where else can you hide? (pause) How do you get around inside your body?"

Step 3: Ask them, "Suppose you were scared, confused, or low in energy; where would you go in your body to feel the most protected and secure? (pause) Go to that place inside your body right now. (pause) What do you see? (pause) What sounds do you hear? (pause) What do you feel like being in this place? (pause) Really get to know this place. (pause) Create in this place all the things you want and need in order to feel relaxed, peaceful, and full of energy. (pause) Let your imagination create everything you want and need there with you."

Step 4: Tell the children, "Now open your eyes and look out at the room around you. (pause) What does the room look like from this place inside you? (pause) What sounds do you hear? (pause) What feeling do you get for the room as you view it from inside?"

Step 5: Finally say, "Now close your eyes and return to your secret hiding place. (pause) When you feel relaxed and refreshed slowly open your eyes, come out of your hiding place, and join us back in this room."

To the Teacher: Let the children share their experiences inside their bodies with the group. Encourage them to talk about what they saw, heard, and felt. Ask them to describe their inner sanctuaries: "What did you take with you to that place so you could feel relaxed, peaceful, and full of energy?"

You can have quiet times during the day when you may want to ask each student to return to his or her secret hiding place. Also, give your students permission to go there when they need to calm themselves, to think about a problem, or to get a boost in energy.

With young children (primary grades) reading the poem "Hiding" by Dorothy Aldis is useful before trying this activity.

ACTIVITY 47—THE AMOEBA

Rationale: This activity illustrates how we are unified and separate at the same time. Experiencing both of these seemingly opposite concepts in one activity helps students to better understand themselves and others.

Step 1: Before starting show your students a motion picture of an amoeba in the processes of cell division (mitosis) and cell multiplication (myosis). If you can't find a motion picture, use a microscope with a slide of an amoeba. If that is not possible, colored pictures of the process will help.

Step 2: Spread out in a large open area. Ask your students to pretend that they are all one cell in the ocean of being, which moves about like a blob. Tell them to imagine they are all part of this one blob that is constantly wiggling, moving, and rolling in, around, and through each other. Have them feel part of this huge amoeba, being aware of what view of the world they have and what sounds they hear.

Step 3: After letting the blob form and move around the room, ring a small bell to signal that the cell is to divide into two amoeba.

Step 4: Have them notice the space between the two amoeba. Each time you ring the bell they are to divide in half again until each student is a single cell. Allow them to be aware of the space they have as single cells. Again ask them to notice the sights, sounds, and feelings of being a separate, single cell. (Note: It is helpful to start with an even number of students, but with each division there may be an uneven number. Have the students as much as possible divide in half each time.)

Step 5: After they have experienced this separate space, ask them to begin the process of joining with another single cell. Again ring the bell each time you want them to multiply, until they have again joined together as one large single cell.

Step 6: Finally, go through cell division once more until they are back to individual single cells.

To the Teacher: You can ask the students to write or talk about this experience afterward. Some themes to focus on are "What different sights, sounds, and feelings did you have as part of the group blob and alone?" "What feelings and sensations did you have while you were separating or joining?" "Was it hard to say good-bye to some who were in your group?" "Was it hard to ask others to join with you again?" "What things did you consider in making these decisions?"

ACTIVITY 48—THE ELEMENTS

Rationale: The purpose of this activity is to help you use your imagination to integrate and balance the four basic elements: earth, wind, fire, and water. You may use appropriate background music, and Paul Horn has recorded a good selection entitled "The Elements" from the album *Inside II.* Use the following instructions:

Step 1: "Lie down on your back and close your eyes. Imagine you are lying on the surface of the earth. (pause) Feel yourself going deep inside the earth all the way to the center of the earth. (pause) Feel yourself moving slowly toward the center of the earth. (pause) What do you see, hear, and feel? Is it hot or cold? Dark or light? Quiet or loud? (pause) Now bring your body back to the surface of the earth again." (Start record here, if you are using "The Elements" recording.)

Step 2: "Imagine that the mountains and oceans and rivers are your body. (pause) Feel all the rocks and soil as part of you. (pause) All the plants and big trees are part of you; see them all as part of your body. (pause) Now feel the animals everywhere as part of you. (pause) Hear them making noises to each other. (pause) Now feel all the people on earth as part of you (pause) everywhere, black, white, red, yellow, and brown, all part of your body."

Step 3: "Now focus in on various parts of you. (pause) For a minute become a tree moving in the breeze. Get up and move as a tree in the wind. (pause) Hear the wind blowing through you; (pause) feel the wind moving your branches."

Step 4: "Now become the wind and move as if you were the wind. Go with the wind to where you want to go. Pretend you are flying with the wind going up over the mountains. (pause) Look down and see the mountains. (pause) Now dive down to the ocean. (pause) Feel its spray against your face and hear the roar of its waves crashing against the shore. (pause) See the deserts and rivers and cities as you travel across the surface of the earth. (pause) Now become like a tornado, (pause) moving, picking up speed, spinning and whirling across the surface of the earth. (pause) Feel your power, listen to your sound, and see yourself gathering up the dust and the buildings as you sweep along. (pause) Now become very light and calm, barely moving at all, (pause) and now perfectly still. (pause)."

Step 5: "Now from your quiet, still place, picture a flame like the flame of a candle. (pause) It is yellow with blue inside the yellow and white inside the blue, just like a candle flame. (pause) Feel it getting warmer and warmer. (pause) Now feel it spreading. (pause) Now see yourself stepping into the flame and becoming a glowing light. (pause) Feel yourself glowing first with yellow light. (pause) Now feel the heaviness of your body, your mind and your feelings burning away in the yellow flame. (pause) You are now free to go deeper into the flame, into the blue of the flame. (pause) Now feel yourself standing inside the white center of the flame, which is very hot and very cold at the same time. (pause) Stand up and become the whole flame dancing and darting and moving. (pause) Everything you touch catches fire and burns. (pause) Hear the crackling of your flame as you burn brightly, full of energy."

Step 6: "As you move and burn, feel the presence of water above you in the clouds that have formed. Begin to feel raindrops hitting you from above, slowly at first, then more strongly, forcing you back to the ground, now pelting you into ashes and spreading you across the ground."

Step 7: "As you feel yourself as smoldering ashes, notice that small particles of you are being carried by a small trickle of water, and now you are flowing down a small ditch being joined by other small trickles as you tumble along. (pause) Soon as you move you can hear the sound of water running faster, and now you are this water, rushing down a mountainside, over rocks, and finally on the valley floor, flowing more slowly and evenly. (pause) As you look from side to side you can see yourself passing various scenes; (pause) small towns, boats, big cities, forests, cliffs, all glide past you as you just flow along. (pause) Now as you look ahead you can see you are entering a great ocean of water. (pause) Feel yourself melt and disappear into the vastness of that ocean. (pause) Now listen; (pause) very quietly within you can hear the sound of the ocean inside your head. (pause) Feel the rhythm of the waves rolling in and washing out to sea again. Move as a wave rolling in on the beach and washing out to sea again."

Step 8: "As you wash up on the beach feel the warmth of the sand and feel yourself evaporating into the air as you roll onto the warm sand. (pause) Feel yourself floating upward toward the sun. (pause) Moving past a few clouds on the way, listen to the sounds as you travel through space; see the lights of deep space flashing by you as you float out into space. (pause–30 seconds) Go out beyond the sun, beyond the stars, beyond the universe itself (pause) [flute solo ends]. Now feel yourself coming back into the universe, floating back, passing the stars and the sun, coming into the atmosphere, passing over the mountains and ocean and back into this class and into your body. (pause) When you are ready open your eyes and look around at all your friends."

To the Teacher: This is a powerful activity, and it may be difficult for your students to share much with others for a while. You may ask them to sit quietly and think about what the experience meant to them before sharing it with others. Since this is a lengthy activity, some break may be appropriate before any sharing occurs.

16

Riding the Cosmic
Roller Coaster

PEAK EXPERIENCES

The term "peak experiences" was applied originally by Abraham Maslow to refer to moments of intense positive feelings, usually involving ecstasy, rapture, bliss, or intense joy. They may also be altered states of consciousness, where everything takes on unreal or surrealistic qualities. Consider the following description by a man with a bowling average of 120 who had just bowled a 230 game: ". . . For some reason, everything was working beautifully—me, the ball, and the pins. . . . At the time it all seemed very unreal. . . . There was no push or force to urge me on—it all began as part of a very relaxed situation. . . . As long as I was relaxed, everything seemed to click, and I could make no mistakes or do nothing wrong. It was an elating experience."[1]

Peak experiences seem to most people to be chance occurrences with no explainable causes, but research into this area indicates the opposite.

[1]Gayle Privette, "Transcendent Functioning: The Full Use of Potentialities," in eds. John Mann and Herbert Otto, *Ways of Growth* (New York: Grossman Publishers, 1968), p. 215.

There are common elements in such experiences, and once a person learns what these elements are he or she should be able to re-create the experiences when he or she wants them. One of the first things to remember about a peak experience is that it is nothing extraordinary. Actually, it is more of a "peek" experience, or a short glimpse at the way things are all the time. The universe is always operating at its peak, and only occasionally do we realize or make real for ourselves this unmistakable fact. A peak experience is a moment when the ego lets go long enough for subconscious core awarenesses to surface. These awarenesses, which Maslow called peak experiences, represent spontaneous flights into transpersonal aliveness. Most of us remain asleep to that level of awareness and are surprised when we suddenly wake up. Unfortunately, we believe these happenings are chance and random occurrences so we go back to sleep again instead of using them to learn how to stay awake.

One of the essential ingredients of peak experiences seems to be a full, clear focus upon an object, such as a task, a problem, or another person. This object seems to stand in sharp contrast to everything else surrounding it, and we usually do not allow ourselves to focus on one object that clearly and fully. We usually move our focus quickly or keep it fuzzy—or we keep our focus on ourselves. Any internal need that remains unfulfilled and demands some amount of attention can block full awareness, as can thinking about past or future events.

There are two ways to facilitate peak experiences: by removing the blocks to awareness and by discovering the common elements in peak experiences. The process of removing barriers to full awareness can be best accomplished through effective interpersonal and intrapersonal communication skills. The following activities are designed to help you and your students remove any remaining barriers and discover the common elements in peak experiences.

ACTIVITY 49—REMOVING BLOCKS TO PEAK AWARENESSES

Rationale: This activity is designed to put you and your students in a state of consciousness where the barriers to peak awarenesses are removed. Activity 49 should be followed closely by Activities 50 and 51, or it can be practiced separately several times before pairing it with the other activities. Barriers will be removed by helping everyone become focused and relaxed.

Step 1: Ask your students to get as comfortable as possible; they can either sit or lie down. Ask them to breathe deeply and slowly imagine that their bodies are like balloons. When they breathe in, the balloon is filled with air and their bodies become tense; when they breathe out, they are empty and limp. If they locate any tense area that won't relax, they should breathe into that area, increasing the tension until they cannot stand it anymore; then they should suddenly relax the area as if their balloons were punctured with a pin. Have them follow this step in any areas where tension is still present.

Step 2: Ask the students to breathe normally and focus on making the in-and-out breaths equal. Have them connect inhalations and exhalations so there is no pause in between. Have them do this step for several minutes until they have established a pattern of evenly connected breathing.

Step 3: Ask them to imagine a bright light above and in front of them, shining on their foreheads. As they breathe in, ask them to imagine the light flowing into their bodies through their foreheads, filling their whole bodies. Ask them to imagine themselves filling up with light from their feet upward.

Step 4: While they are completing Step 3, ask them to pay attention to their thoughts. Ask them to imagine that their minds are a lake, with the wind blowing across the surface, causing thoughts to appear as ripples. Gradually, the wind dies down and the surface of the lake becomes clear and calm.

Step 5: Ask them to continue calming their minds, and now add instructions for deeper relaxation. Ask them to say "I am" to themselves as they inhale and "at peace" as they exhale.

To the Teacher: This activity or a similar one for deep relaxation is usually necessary to quiet the conscious mind and body and allow the subconscious to emerge. Direct access to the subconscious is a necessary ingredient for producing so-called peak experiences.

ACTIVITY 50—PEAK STIMULI SELECTION[2]

Rationale: Peak stimuli are your favorite things to smell, taste, touch, look at, and listen to. These are the major sensory modes that people use to incorporate experiences, and therefore, are the most direct elements of a peak experience. It is important that your students take their time to select the things they like the *very most*. The closer they come to the favorite things, the more use they will be able to make of the information.

Step 1: Ask your students to fill out the following inventory of peak stimuli:

a. List the three things that you enjoy smelling the most.

1. _____ 2. _____ 3. _____

b. List the three things that you enjoy tasting the most.

1. _____ 2. _____ 3. _____

c. List the three things that you enjoy touching the most.

1. _____ 2. _____ 3. _____

d. List the three things that you enjoy looking at the most.

1. _____ 2. _____ 3. _____

Note: In a group, you as the leader should select the background music. Make your choices from those suggested by the students or your own favorites; also, some suggested recordings are "Love-Death" and "Prelude" from *Tristan and Isolde, Inside Taj Mahal* by Paul Horn, *Köln Concert* by Keith Jarrett, Pacibel's *Canon in D*.

Step 2: Ask your students to bring to class one item for each of the five senses. If they originally selected items that cannot be brought into class (e.g., smelling the sea air), they may add new items now. It is important that you give them the time to gather all their items, which do not have to have any relationship to each other as long as there is one for each sense.

Step 3: Have them sit with their peak stimuli with their eyes closed.

[2]Adapted from a similar exercise by Paul Bindrim, "Facilitating Peak Experiences," in eds. John Mann and Herbert Otto, *Ways of Growth* (New York: Grossman Publishers, 1968), pp. 116–26.

Ask them to smell, taste, and touch them, all while imagining that they are looking at their favorite visual stimulus. Ask them to imagine all these sensations flowing into their body through their foreheads and moving to the peaceful center of their being. Have them continue to let the sensations flow in, filling and overflowing with their pleasant joy. As they do so, play a classical or semiclassical recording at moderately high volume. Ravel's *Bolero* or "Prelude" to *Tristan and Isolde* are good because they begin quietly and build to a climax.

To the Teacher: This activity is quite effective for encouraging sensory inputs necessary for peak experiences. You could ask the students to create a scene with these stimuli, generating their own peak experiences in fantasy. Usually the peak stimuli themselves produce the desired effect.

ACTIVITY 51—FACILITATING PEAK EXPERIENCES[3]

Rationale: Research has shown that individuals do tend to have consistent patterns in their peak experiences, which can be defined as times of great happiness and pleasure where you were filled with delight. They are the happiest moments of your life! Knowing that all of them occurred in the mountains, for example, a person could plan activities there.

Step 1: After describing as completely as possible what a peak experience is, have your students write down as many of them as they can remember. Tell them to write down a few key words, like "Watching sunset on beach with F.," for each experience.

Step 2: Have them divide into subgroups of two or three, where members share their peak experiences. Following each person's sharing, the small group should help each other identify his or her patterns.

Step 3: Ask your students to list ways they could use these common elements to seek additional peak experiences. Ask them to develop a plan to create more opportunities for them (e.g., "I am going to plan a trip to the mountains during the Aspen autumn").

Step 4: Ask them to re-experience one of their peak experiences. Ask them to imagine the event as if it were happening for the first time, as

---

[3]Adapted from a similar exercise by Herbert Otto, *Group Methods to Actualize Human Potential* (Beverly Hills, Cal.: The Holistic Press, 1970), pp. 253–59.

though the experience were entirely new. Tell them to look at the scene and allow it to emerge, and not to try to remember it. Ask them if they hear any sounds coming from the persons or things they are seeing. Tell them to pay attention to any smells or aromas and to feel sensations coming from their bodies. Add any other instructions you think will help them get into the experience. When you think sensory contact has been established remain silent, letting your students flow with the experience.

Step 5: Tell them when they are ready to leave the scene they should open their eyes and return to the room. Ask each person, if time permits, to share his or her experience.

To the Teacher: During the sharing there is a tendency for class members to reach even higher peaks. Plan time for sharing and let it emerge naturally. Some students may be unable to share much immediately; let them join in later, if they want.

THE POWER OF UNCONDITIONAL LOVE

When you transcend the struggles of the ego to define itself and exercise power and control over the reality you have created, you reach a place where unconditional love is possible. Even if you have escaped all the ego traps along the way, you will still have to learn how to love unconditionally. Most of us believe that we must in some way earn love before we can have it and that others must behave in certain ways before they deserve our love. From this position, your well-intentioned attempts to give or receive love usually end up in separation and alienation instead of a joyous union of spirits.

Unconditional love honors and accepts the transpersonal reality that at our core we are alike; we are one. Unconditional love is simply accepting yourself and everyone else totally and completely. First, you must learn to love yourself unconditionally in the here and now. The more you learn to love and accept yourself totally and unconditionally, the more you realize that everything you do is helping you develop effective skills in transpersonal communication.

Everything you do is an effective or ineffective attempt to find unconditional love and communicate transpersonally. Even if someone gets angry and yells at you, it is an opportunity for you to learn how to love and accept unconditionally. If you use your ego to deal with the situation, you may judge the other person as "wrong" and therefore separate from you. The truth is that you have either done the same thing as the other person or wanted to do the same thing at some time in your life. So you can look at everything that happens to you on a continuum from total separateness to total oneness. Your thoughts and actions that separate you from others are at the lower end of the continuum, and those that unite you with others are at the higher end. Thus everything you think or do can be evaluated on the basis of whether it makes you feel more separate from yourself and others or more loving and united.

Nothing really limits you except your thoughts. When you improve the quality of your thoughts your life will begin to give evidence of its natural and limitless possibilities.

Paranoia is the experience of being separated and alienated from your inner core and from the inner core of others. The opposite of paranoia is harmonia, or being connected and unified with your inner core and that of others. The process of learning to live the power of unconditional love involves removing your paranoid, negative thoughts and replacing them with harmonoid, positive thoughts and feelings. The Navaho's have a greeting, which translates to "I greet the highest in you." This greeting represents a way of making contact with your highest thoughts and feelings.

ACTIVITY 52—ACCEPTING YOURSELF

Rationale: One of the main ingredients of unconditional love is self-acceptance. When you can accept yourself unconditionally, you will have cleared away some of the major barriers to your connection with your inner core and that of others. Your attacks against those things you don't like in yourself keep yourself separated and alienated from your true loving nature.

Step 1: Ask your students to make a list of three things they don't like about themselves. They can include physical features (overweight, too short, etc.), personality traits (shy, not very smart, etc.) or things they can't do (I can't sing, learn math, etc.).

Step 2: Ask them to take each of their negative self-statements and turn it into a positive statement of acceptance. At first, suggest they use this method: Write "I now accept myself as _____." (For example, "I now accept myself as overweight.")

Step 3: After the students take each negative statement and turn it into a positive one, tell them to write any related negative thoughts that still keep them from self-acceptance. For example, if one wrote "I now accept myself as overweight," and his or her negative thoughts immediately afterward were something like, "Other people won't accept me if I'm overweight," then he or she needs to convert that negative thought into a positive one. He or she might write, "The more I accept myself, the more other people will accept me." After the students write this new statement, they need to listen again for negative thoughts, converting them to positive statements until no more negative thoughts arise. They can then go back to the original accepting statement and rewrite it or rewrite any other of their positive statements. When they can write the statements repeatedly (five to ten times) without any negative interference, then they know that it has been removed.

To the Teacher: It is preferable to take only one statement at a time and work with that one until it is clear. Also, the first time you use this method be sure to model the process, using some visual aids to help make it clear and concrete. Some individual tutoring may be necessary at first for some students. You can ask those students who have learned the process to assist those who are having difficulty with it.

ACTIVITY 53—THE UNIVERSE ALWAYS SAYS YES

Rationale: This activity helps you see that your thoughts manifest themselves in your life. If you think negative thoughts, you will create negative experiences. Also, this activity will help you remove "wants" as a barrier to obtaining them. To understand this idea, you must remember that to whatever you are thinking, the universe says "yes." For example, if you think you have trouble understanding math, the universe will say "yes, you do have trouble understanding math"; or if you think you are smart, the universe will say "yes, you are smart." If you say, "I want to be good at math," the universe will say, "yes, you want to be good at math." Therefore, wanting something can become a barrier to having it; to continue to "want" something does not set up the thought pattern necessary for getting it. A statement that dissolves the "wanting barrier" is "I am now good at math."

Step 1: Ask your students to choose a partner and look him or her in the eye. One of the pair is to play the role of the universe, which is to say "yes" or "I agree" to everything his or her partner says. The other partner is instructed to tell the universe what he or she wants. For example, someone might say, "I want to have more friends." Start by having each student share three wants, and then have them switch roles.

Step 2: Each person must restate each of his or her "wants" so that they can be manifested. Have the students say each want to their partners as if they had already obtained it. For example, instead of saying "I want to have more friends," the student will say, "I have all the friends I want." Partners who are playing the universe should reply, "Yes, [your name], you now do have all the friends you want." Do this step with each of the three wants, and then have the partners switch roles.

Step 3: This step involves processing out any negative thoughts to which the universe can also say "yes." These thoughts may prevent positive wants from manifesting themselves. Have each person report any negative thoughts that surfaced as they completed Step 2, taking each of the negative thoughts and turning it into a positive statement. For example, if you thought that people you want as friends wouldn't want to be friends with you, verbalize this thought to your partner and then change it into a positive statement, like "The people I choose as friends also choose me." Make this statement to the universe, and your partner should reply, "That's right" or with a similar affirming statement.

To the Teacher: This is an important clearing activity that helps your students get what they want. Whenever a student thinks he or she cannot get what he or she wants, use this activity.

ACTIVITY 54—UNCONDITIONAL SELF-AFFIRMING LOVE

Rationale: When you can affirm yourself as coming from your inner core, you are able to love yourself totally and unconditionally. Most of us have denied our inner core and have placed conditions on our ability to love and be loved. This activity is designed to clear out those conditions set up by your ego so you can have a direct experience with your inner core, where unconditional love resides.

Step 1: Ask your students to pair off and sit facing each other. Taking turns, each is to repeat the following statement for five minutes: "I have all the love in the universe all of the time." Tell them to look their partners in the eyes and to keep repeating the self-affirming statement. Partners should acknowledge the statement by saying things like "Yes, that's right" or "I agree." After five minutes, the students should switch roles and repeat the process.

Step 2: The person who started now repeats to his or her partner what was said in Step 1. He or she would say "[name], you have all the love in the universe all of the time." Parthers should acknowledge the message by saying things like "Yes, I do." After five minutes, the students should switch roles and repeat the process.

To the Teacher: This consciousness-clearing activity can be repeated periodically to help keep negative thoughts from dominating. Older students or students who have used this technique before can verbalize their negative thoughts as they are repeating or hearing the self-affirming statements.

ACTIVITY 55—FORGIVING OTHERS

Rationale: There is less opportunity to be in contact with your inner core if you are harboring negative thoughts about yourself or other people. Forgiveness turns out to be a major pathway to unconditional love. Forgiving yourself or others is a gift you can give yourself, because it removes one of the major barriers between you and your inner core and that of others. When you forgive, you remove unnecessary fear, guilt, and pain that keep you separate from yourself and others.

Step 1: Ask your students to close their eyes and think of people they don't like or are angry at for some reason. These people, or incidents involving them, can be current or from the past. Have the students picture each one of the persons in their minds. Have them pay attention briefly to their thoughts and feelings about each of the persons as they visualize them.

Step 2: Now have the students open their eyes and make a list of these people, writing their thoughts and feelings about each person under his or her name.

Step 3: Have them write the following statement for each of the people on their list: "My negative thoughts and feelings about [name of person] are keeping me from being in contact with my loving nature which resides in my inner core."

Step 4: Now ask them to write the following statement for each of the people on their list: "Because of my loving nature it is now easy to forgive [name of person] for all that I accused him or her of doing to me."

Step 5: Finally, ask them to close their eyes and see each of the persons in their minds. Ask them to look at each person for a while until they can see some light coming from the person somewhere, a little gleam that they hadn't noticed in this person before. Tell them to find some little spark of brightness shining through the ugly picture of this person that they previously had. Have them keep looking at their picture of the person until they see a light shining somewhere within him or her. Then ask them to have the light spread out until it covers the person and makes him or her look radiant and beautiful. Have them follow this step with each person on their list.

To the Teacher: This is a powerful activity for your students to learn. When they begin to understand how forgiving people helps remove barriers to their own love, they are well on their way to taking responsibility for their own thoughts and feelings. If students are having trouble seeing this relationship, perhaps a discussion of the topic may help. Ask them to list what benefits they and others derive from not forgiving others. Then ask them to list the benefits if they did forgive others. Compare the lists. Usually it is clear that the benefits of not forgiving are not as tangible as the others.

ACTIVITY 56—FORGIVING YOURSELF

Rationale: After you have forgiven others you are free to remove a remaining barrier to unconditional love: your nonforgiveness of yourself. Forgiving yourself is a demonstration of unconditional love, a way of validating who you really are instead of what your ego made up about who you are. When you haven't forgiven yourself you are open to attack by your own thoughts.

Step 1: Ask your students to close their eyes and think about all the mistakes they have made or things for which they are angry at themselves. Ask them to develop a picture of themselves, using all the things they don't like about themselves and things they use to be angry at themselves.

Step 2: After they have developed their negative pictures of themselves, ask them to open their eyes and make a list of things they don't like and are angry at.

Step 3: Ask them to write the following statement for each of the things on their list: "By not forgiving myself of _____ I am keeping myself blind to my basic loving nature."

Step 4: Now ask them to write the following statement about each of the items on their list: "Because of my basic loving nature it is now easy to forgive myself for _____."

Step 5: Finally, ask them to close their eyes and picture themselves. Ask them to look at themselves until they can see light coming from somewhere in their bodies. Tell them to find a spark of brightness shining through the negative picture of themselves they held previously. When they see light, tell them to have the light spread out until it covers their bodies. Then ask them to picture themselves as radiantly beautiful and perfect; free from any weaknesses or limitations.

To the Teacher: This activity can be used with an entire class or individually with students who are resentful and angry. If students are having trouble visualizing themselves, have them look in a full-length mirror for Steps 1 and 5.

ACTIVITY 57—THOUGHT IMPROVEMENT

Rationale: This activity emphasizes improving the quality of your thoughts to learn to manifest unconditional love. The practice of thought improvement can extend the experience of unconditional love to all aspects of your life. Since we have over 50,000 thoughts a day, there is plenty of time to practice this skill.

Step 1: Ask your students to spend ten minutes a day watching their thoughts. Have them sit comfortably with their eyes closed and simply notice each thought during that time. They are not to evaluate or change their thoughts, but just watch them go by.

Step 2: After ten minutes of practice ask them to open their eyes. Now ask them to interject the following thought after every other thought they have: Say "We are" when inhaling and "one" when exhaling. For example, a sequence might be as follows: "This will make the activity more concrete: [inhale] We are [exhale] one; I hope this is clear [We are one]."

Step 3: Ask your students to practice thought improvement for a period of time each day until they can do it whenever they want.

To the Teacher: This thought should eventually be like a mantra that can be repeated at any time or can operate in the background of your mind as a constant for all your other thoughts. When this goal happens you will always be in contact with your inner core and the inner core of others.

17

Journey
Beyond the Self

THERAPEUTIC RITUALS

What are the things you do the same or in a similar way almost every day as part of your daily routine? These are called daily rituals, and they may vary from the way you wake up in the morning to what you do while driving to work. They are activities that can have positive, neutral, or negative effects on how you experience your day. For example, what do you do when you wake up in the morning? Trace your activities from the time you wake up until you leave for work. You may discover that without giving it much thought, you have created positive and enjoyable rituals to help you start the day. If you find some rituals that seem to have neutral or negative effects, you can begin to search for more positive rituals to replace them.

As you and your students begin changing your communication patterns, you may have already developed new therapeutic rituals. A therapeutic ritual is a daily activity that has positive, therapeutic effects on those who use it. Many of the activities in this book can be used as therapeutic rituals on a daily basis in your classroom, for example, training in concentration, centering, and energy awareness.

For transpersonal communication, we must develop daily rituals that help support our core connectedness with each other and our environment. Core connectedness involves the sense of being fully alive to the realities of the present moment. It is the realization of our basic connections with self, others, and the cosmos.

Only when transpersonal communication is practiced on a daily basis are the real benefits going to emerge—which is why therapeutic rituals are important as part of the process of integrating your new patterns of communication.

The following Daily Ritual Analysis Chart[1] can be used to increase your awareness of daily rituals, their effects on you, and how you can change those that have neutral or negative effects.

DAILY RITUAL ANALYSIS CHART

Date_____

Identifying information:

Age _____ Sex _____ Marital Status _____ Living Status: (alone, children, etc.) _____.

A daily ritual is an activity that you do the same or in a similar way almost every day. The activity can have positive, neutral, or negative effects on your life.

Instructions: Below are a number of common categories of daily rituals. Under each category, list and describe the daily rituals you are aware of. Then by checking the appropriate column(s) on the right, indicate some additional characteristics of your rituals. A suggested way to begin is to trace what you typically do from the time you get up until you go to bed.

---

[1]This instrument was developed by Barry K. Weinhold and Marge Theeman, who are doing research on therapeutic rituals.

	Category	Primary Focus	Effects of the Ritual
Name of Ritual	Description (Be specific—what do you do?)	Alone/With Others	+ = Positive 0 = Neutral − = Negative
Hygiene Rituals	Bathing, shaving, brushing teeth, etc.		
Waking-Up Rituals	(What do you do routinely to wake up before you get out of bed?)		
Food-Related Rituals	Eating, food shopping, etc.		
Transportation Rituals	Driving to work or taking the bus.		
Work- or School-Related Rituals	(Things you do daily at work or school)		
Relaxed Time Rituals	(What do you do to relax?)		
Sleeping Rituals	(How much sleep? How do you get to sleep? etc.)		
Others Not Included Above			

Instructions: Please respond to the following questions.

1. Which of your daily rituals has the most positive effects?

_____

_____

2. Which of your daily rituals has the most negative effects?

_____

_____

3. What changes in daily rituals would help you the most?

_____

_____

4. What new rituals would you like to add to your daily routines?

_____

_____

ACTIVITY 58—CHANGING YOUR DAILY RITUALS

Rationale: This activity involves using the Daily Ritual Analysis Chart with your students to help them learn how to change unwanted rituals. Bringing your daily activities into harmony with your new communication patterns is an important way to support your growth.

Step 1: Have your students fill out the chart themselves and bring it to class for discussion.

Step 2: Ask them to choose a partner and exchange charts. Ask partners to go over the chart to make sure they understand what is written on the other person's chart, asking for clarification when needed.

Step 3: Ask them to write a daily ritual they would like to change on a card, without signing their names.

Step 4: You or one of your students collects the cards and reads them to the class. The task of the class is to suggest a number of ways to change the ritual listed. (*Note:* To save some time in this step, you can divide a large group into smaller groups of six to eight students.)

Step 5: Ask each student to design a new daily ritual to replace the unwanted one. Caution them to select daily rituals they can change without forcing others to make corresponding changes. An example of the latter would be to practice concentration training at breakfast or dinner time and thus miss the meal.

Step 6: It is important to have each student make a public statement of his or her new ritual. The students could simply tell the group what they are going to do, asking for what they want from others in the way of support. Or they may wish to write the statement and post it on a bulletin board designed especially for this purpose.

To the Teacher: Encourage your students to start small with this activity so they can experience success. Urge them to choose a ritual to change when they have built-in support or where they have a good chance of succeeding.

ACTIVITY 59—THE DANCE OF DAILY LIFE

Rationale: Movement and dance can be used to help your students experience their daily rituals and share them with each other.

Step 1: Have your students form small groups of six to eight. Start by having them share the results of their Daily Ritual Analysis Charts, particularly noting the variety of daily rituals.

Step 2: Use a recording of congo drums as background music, or if you have talented students in your class, ask them to create the dance rhythms. Ask each member of the small group to create his or her own dance of daily life by acting out the daily rituals he or she has identified.

Step 3: Now ask each small group to develop fantasies and to draw pictures representing a new ritual that emphasizes core connectedness.

Step 4: Ask each small group to develop and perform their fantasy dance before the large group.

Step 5: The final step involves weaving each fantasy dance into a total group dance that emphasizes core connectedness.

To the Teacher: A congo drum rhythm or a fast 4/4 beat is usually good background music for this activity. If you can get marimbas and percussion instruments from your band or orchestra director, you can use your students as accompanying musicians.

Obviously this is a high-energy activity, and some counter-balancing quiet activity may be used to follow it.

This activity is best done where you have plenty of space in which to move around. A gymnasium is ideal. Also, during the individual and small-group dances, the rest of the class can join in by rhythmic clapping and by forming a double line or circle around the dancers.

KEEPING A JOURNAL AS A THERAPEUTIC RITUAL

Keeping a journal and diary have been used for centuries to track one's thoughts, feelings, and behavior over a period of time. Many famous writers and scientists have used a daily journal or diary to store ideas and insights. Jonas Salk, the inventor of the Salk vaccine for polio credits his journal as the source of his discovery. Keeping personal journals was also important to religious persons who valued the reality of inner experience.

A personal journal can be a valuable way of recording and then evaluating one's progress toward certain goals; thus it becomes a self-testing instrument. Because it helps you focus on a particular goal or series of events, it also can be a self-limiting activity. This is an important consideration in using a journal as therapeutic ritual to support change and growth. A way to avoid this pitfall is to develop specific procedures and different journals for different purposes.

Keeping a journal as a tool for transpersonal communication requires that you help your students learn ways to tap into their transpersonal core. Even though, as individuals, our lives are separate, through our core experiences we can reach into the underground pool of transpersonal experience. We have to reach deep within ourselves to find the underground pool, and journal keeping can be one way of doing it. The following activities are designed to meet specific transpersonal objectives.

ACTIVITY 60—KEEPING A DAILY JOURNAL

Rationale: The discipline of learning to keep a daily journal is an important first step to more extensive uses of it. A daily journal most closely resembles a diary. The purpose of it is to develop a running account of your important subjective experiences each day, source material for more extensive journal-keeping activities.

Step 1: Ask your students to set aside a certain time during their day to make entries in their journal. The best times are at the end of the day or shortly after waking up in the morning.

Step 2: Have your students use concentration training before writing as a way of quieting the external noises and opening up to their deeper awarenesses.

Step 3: Ask them to close their eyes and go back in their memories to the past twenty-four hours. Ask them to let themselves feel the inner movement of the events in their lives over the previous day.

Step 4: Ask them to wait until they have a feel for their previous day and then to open their eyes and record whatever they can recall. Urge them not to censor or judge but merely describe. Also urge them to keep their entries brief and not to be concerned about grammar or literary style.

Step 5: After they have completed their daily entries, ask them to reread what they wrote and sit quietly for a few minutes, feeling their emotions. Have them ask themselves, "What am I feeling about what I wrote?" "What are the important feelings that emerge from what I wrote?" Then ask them to record whatever additional feelings, thoughts, or observations they wish.

To the Teacher: You may want to work with the art department and have your students design their own journals.

ACTIVITY 61—LIFE-PERIOD JOURNAL

Rationale: A life period is a recent unit of time that has some significance in a person's present life. The purpose of a life-period journal is to pull together thoughts and feelings from a recent period, for example, a school year, summer vacation, new job, or move to a new place.

Step 1: Ask your students to close their eyes and realize their feelings in the present.

Step 2: Ask them to draw a large circle on an 8½″ by 11″ sheet of paper and then subdivide the circle into four quadrants. Ask them to write a current feeling in each of the four quadrants.

Step 3: Ask them to write two sentences about one of the feelings to elaborate on its meaning.

Step 4: Have them now begin to identify the characteristics of a recent life period. Ask them to close their eyes and think about the following questions: "Where did your present life period begin?" "What event or events mark the beginning?" "What are the main features of this life period?"

Step 5: Ask the students to sit with their eyes closed and begin to feel the inner movement of their recent life experiences without judging them. (Have them use the thought-watching activity to observe their thoughts.)

Step 6: As images, thoughts, and feelings emerge, instruct the students to begin recording them.

Step 7: Ask the students to complete the following sentence: "This life period has been like a. . . ." Tell them to use any similes or metaphors that seem to fit.

Step 8: Step 7 ends the preliminary steps. Now have your students focus on the specifics of their life periods. Ask them to write when the period began; what event marked its beginning; what memories, inner experiences, relationships, dreams, and/or other significant events come to mind. Ask them to describe them briefly in their journals.

Step 9: Now ask them to close their eyes again and reflect on what they wrote. Ask them to recapture the inner continuity and movement of the recent life period, and have them focus on its meaning for them in their present situation.

Step 10: After giving them time to reflect on the meaning of this period, ask them to make additional entries in their life-period journals.

To the Teacher: The life-period journal is a good way to put students in touch with the movement and flow of events in their lives. Students can use it on their own when they need it, and you can reuse the activity from time to time. It is useful to help students integrate material you covered over a particular time period.

ACTIVITY 62—JOURNAL OF
TRANSPERSONAL DIALOGUE

Rationale: This journal is designed to help people make contact with their transpersonal core and sort out the larger meanings from their life experiences.

Step 1: Using Activity 51 have your students go over those experiences that had a profound effect upon them and helped them make contact with their transpersonal core.

Step 2: Ask them to list the experiences in chronological order and read the list several times to themselves, taking note of the feelings and thoughts that arise as they read. Have them enter these thoughts in their journals.

Step 3: Now ask the students to think back to the persons who were important to them in a profound, meaningful way at the time of each of the experiences. Ask them to include, not only those they had a personal relationship with, but also people like writers, politicians, and spiritual figures who helped them make contact with their transpersonal core and provided a deep and direct experience of knowing.

Step 4: From the various people they identified, ask your students to choose one to have an imaginary conversation with. Ask your students to visualize the person, feel his or her presence, and listen for some words from him or her.

Step 5: Ask your students, who are sitting with their eyes closed, to greet silently their friend and tell him or her the meaning of the relationship to them. Ask them to tell this person why they have called upon him or her and what they want to ask.

Step 6: Ask your students to carry on a dialogue with their friend while sitting quietly and write it in their journals as they do so. Instruct your students to remain open to whatever information they receive without making any judgments.

Step 7: Then allow time for your students to share their experiences with the group. Ask them to respond to open-ended sentences like "As a result of my dialogue, I learned that . . ." or "As a result of my dialogue, I was surprised that. . . ."

To the Teacher: Leave ample time for the dialogue. Several times students will pause, although they are not finished. These pauses enable the students to collect their thoughts, and often when the dialogue resumes it is at a deeper level. Encourage your students to stay open even during the pauses.

18

The Collective Self and the Myth of Aloneness

One of the popular myths we have supported is that at our core we are all alone and separate from everyone and everything. This is an illusion that the ego has created to protect itself. We work really hard to define our separateness. We focus on our differences, and by concentrating our conscious thoughts on these differences, we create them. To maintain this myth or illusion we develop numerous mechanisms. One is the creation of an enormous power structure where someone always has more power than someone else. All our major relationships are defined in terms of power, and everyone ends up being more powerful than someone else and at the same time less powerful than others. This tactic helps us maintain the illusion of difference and separateness. It also helps us believe that someone else, because of their power-related qualities, knows what is best for us more than we do. We tend to use this power structure to create a "need-obligate system" in relationships, where we act as if we need someone else's power to tell us if we are lovable and capable. This other-directedness keeps our focus away from contact with our own inner core. Research on this way of relating suggests that the need for approval from others is the most common block to transcending ego functioning. We also use guilt and resentment as mechanisms to support the myth of aloneness.

This self-deception is not a deliberate attempt to harm ourselves and others. It is simply an adaptation by the ego in its attempts to make sense and order out of the world. The ego becomes strengthened in this process, and as it gets stronger the possibility of transcending its functioning becomes both exciting and frightening.

The transpersonal aspects of our behavior generally are not supported or strengthened in our society. We are unfamiliar with ourselves at the deepest levels of our being. The activities in this book are designed to remove some of the barriers to awareness of your transpersonal core and provide opportunities for you and your students to strengthen and support these core awarenesses. Part of the task is learning how to operate in the world while still maintaining contact with your transpersonal core. This aspect takes courage and practice.

The support for the collective self can come from many sources. One important source is nature, in which everything is clearly connected. By being aware of the unity in everything, you can receive much needed support for your own connection with everyone and everything. We can also begin to look beneath the artificial differences your ego generally creates in relating to others and see how you are connected at deeper levels of functioning. Every time you meet or talk to someone you have a chance to practice this way of communicating or relating.

Transpersonal communication allows you to relate to yourself and other people at deeper levels. As with any set of skills, the more you practice the better you will get. This book's activities and suggested ways to use the skills within the regular curriculum provide suggestions on how to practice. We hope that these will only serve to stimulate your creative thoughts so you can create many more ways to nurture and support your deepest levels of functioning. The following Self-Survey on Transpersonal Communication may help you to determine with how much of your transpersonal self you have made contact and to support further your continued search.

SELF-SURVEY ON
TRANSPERSONAL COMMUNICATION

Directions: Place a check mark in the column that best represents your perception of yourself. Please answer every item.

	Never	Sometimes	Usually	Always
1. I am aware of when I am walking from center or off-center.				
2. I can dissolve my major barriers by changing negative thoughts into positive affirmations.				
3. I am easily distracted from what I am doing by things going on around me.				
4. I tend to spend time thinking about my reactions to things that happened in my recent past.				
5. I allow other people to drain my energy.				
6. I have a hard time relaxing my mind and body.				
7. I practice some form of meditation.				
8. I keep a daily written journal of my activities, thoughts, and feelings.				
9. I use some form of physical exercise that combines mind and body conditioning (e.g., yoga, aikido, Tai Chi, etc.).				
10. I have trouble remembering my dreams.				
11. I have difficulty loving myself when I make mistakes.				
12. I feel basically alone and separate from others.				
13. I am in touch with my basic core feelings of love.				
14. I am able to facilitate my own peak experiences.				

	Never	Sometimes	Usually	Always
15. When I am feeling low in energy I have difficulty generating energy for myself.				
16. I am able to share my energy freely with others.				
17. I realize that what I like and dislike in others is a projection of how I feel about myself.				
18. I have trouble understanding the difference between looking at something and seeing it.				
19. I am aware of energy flowing through my body.				
20. I trust my intuitive thoughts and feelings.				

_____ + _____ + _____ + _____ = _____

Total
Score

Scoring Procedures: Each item is weighted 1, 2, 3, or 4. Certain items are keyed with the "Always" column, weighted at 4, and others with the "Never" column, also weighted at 4. The following key shows how to score each item:

Items scored 1, 2, 3, 4 (Never = 1 and Always = 4) include numbers 2, 7, 8, 9, 13, 14, 16, 17, 19, 20.

Items scored 4, 3, 2, 1 (Never = 4 and Always = 1) include numbers 1, 3, 4, 5, 6, 10, 11, 12, 15, 18.

Write the appropriate number in the column where you placed a check mark. Add all the numbers in each column and add the sums of each column to get a total score. Place your score on the continuum below and look at the interpretation that fits your category.

---

20   50   80

20–29   rigid ego boundaries
30–39   some small cracks in the ego boundaries beginning to appear
40–49   willing to recognize transpersonal aspects
50–59   should keep practicing transpersonal communication skills
60–69   evidence of effective transpersonal communication skills
70+   all systems are go

COMMON ERRORS IN
TRANSPERSONAL COMMUNICATION

1. Mistaking unity and sameness. Being connected or unified with others and your environment does not mean you are the same as everyone else. As you experience your connectedness you gain access to the deep levels of yourself. Basically this concept is a koan (paradox) or riddle: Out of unity comes diversity.

2. Experiencing your head as your physical center. Many people tend to operate from their heads and begin to lose contact with the rest of their bodies.

3. Distrusting intuitive thoughts.

4. Seeing yourself as different from others, alienated and separate.

5. Tending to view your imagination as nonproductive.

6. Trying to get energy from other sources when needing energy; unable to energize yourself without the help of others.

7. Inability to share energy freely with others.

8. Easily drawn off center by reactions of others.

9. Inability to quiet your mind. Thoughts crowd in, interfering with concentration. You may be thinking of one thing, and other conflicting thoughts keep interfering.

10. Tending to have major barriers embedded in negative, limiting thought patterns.

11. Viewing a peak experience as something that "just happens"; not realizing you can facilitate your own peak experiences.

ON THE PLANET, EARTH, SEPTEMBER, 1969
THE UNANIMOUS DECLARATION OF
INTERDEPENDENCE

When in the course of Evolution it becomes necessary for one species to denounce the notion of independence from all the rest, and to assume among the powers of the earth, the interdependent station to which the natural laws of the cosmos have placed them, a decent respect for the opinions of all mankind requires that they should declare the conditions which impel them to assert their interdependence.

We hold these truths to be self-evident, that all species have evolved with equal and unalienable rights, that among these are Life, Liberty, and the Pursuit of Happiness.—That to insure these rights, nature has instituted certain principles for the sustenance of all species, deriving these principles from the capabilities of the planet's life-support system.—That whenever any behavior by members of one species becomes destructive of these principles it is the function of other members of that species to alter or abolish such behavior and to re-establish the theme of interdependence with all life, in such a form and in accordance with those natural principles, that will effect their safety and happiness. Prudence, indeed, will dictate that cultural values long established should not be altered for light and transient causes. Mankind is more disposed to suffer from asserting a vain notion of independence than to right themselves by abolishing that culture to which they are now accustomed.—But when a long train of abuses and insurpations of these principles of interdependence evinces a subtle design to reduce them, through absolute despoliation of the planet's fertility to a state of ill will, bad health, and great anxiety, it is their right, it is their duty, to throw off such notions of independence from other species and from the life-support system, and to provide new guards for the re-establishment of the security and maintenance of these principles. Such has been the quiet and patient sufferage of all the species, and such is now the necessity which constrains the species Homo Sapiens to reassert the principles of interdependence.—The history of the present notion of independence is a history of repeated injuries and usurpations all having in direct effect the establishment of an absolute tyranny over life.

To prove this let facts be submitted to a candid world.

(1) People have refused to recognize the roles of other species and the importance of natural principles for growth of the food they require. (2) People have refused to recognize that they are interacting with other species in an evolutionary process. (3) People have fouled the waters that all

176

life partakes of. (4) People have transformed the face of the earth to enhance their notion of independence from it, and in so doing have interrupted many natural processes that they are dependent upon. (5) People have contaminated the common household with substances that are foreign to the life process, which are causing many organisms great difficulties. (6) People have massacred and made extinct fellow species for their feathers and furs, for their skins and tusks. (7) People have persecuted most persistently those known as coyote, lion, wolf, and fox because of their dramatic role in the expression of interdependence. (8) People are proliferating in such an irresponsible manner as to threaten the survival of all species. (9) People have warred upon one another, which has brought great sorrow to themselves and vast destruction to the homes and the food supplies of many living things. (10) People have denied others the right to live to completion their interdependencies to the full extent of their capabilities.

We, therefore, among the mortal representatives of the eternal process of life and evolutionary principles, in mutual humbleness explicitly stated, appealing to the ecological consciousness of the world for the rectitude of our intentions, do solemnly publish and declare that all species are interdependent; that they are all free to realize these relationships to the full extent of their capabilities; that each species is subservient to the requirements of the natural processes that sustain all life. We, therefore, support this declaration with a firm reliance on all other members of our species who understand their consciousness as a capability, to assist all of us and our brothers to interact in order to realize a life process that manifests its maximum potential of diversity, vitality, and planetary fertility to ensure the continuity of life on earth.[1]

[1]Clifford C. Humphrey, Director *Ecology Action Education Institute*, Modesto, Cal. Reprinted by permission.

19

How to Integrate Transpersonal Communication Skills into the Regular Curriculum

This chapter contains four examples of how to teach various subject matters in the regular curriculum by using some of the transpersonal communication skills presented in the previous six chapters. We encourage you to adapt our examples to fit your particular classroom and to develop additional materials that integrate other transpersonal communication skills into the curriculum.

In general, a transpersonal communications approach involves a search for core understandings that reach deep within the individual. This kind of learning is indeed profound and can last a lifetime. These journeys into the core self can occur as a result of interaction with almost every kind of subject matter. Poetry, literature, art, science, mathematics, history, physical education, and all other subjects can offer rich opportunities for students to make contact with their cores. All that is missing is a creative, sensitive teacher who knows how to facilitate these experiences through whatever subject matter they happen to have mastered.

TEACHING LEARNING SKILLS
IN THE PRIMARY GRADES
BY USING CONCENTRATION

A child's ability to concentrate is directly related to his or her ability to learn. Concentration helps students not only to acquire knowledge but also to integrate the facts and information they learn.

The earlier children acquire concentration skills, the more open they will be to the learning process in subsequent years. In fact, concentration is perhaps the most important aspect of the learning process and a skill that allows children to learn pretty much what they choose and at their own rate.

As all of us know, the attention span (or ability to concentrate) of most young children tends to be very limited. Perhaps we have too readily assumed that they are *unable* to concentrate for longer periods of time. Their seeming inability actually may be related to a lack of training in concentration.

Purpose: To help primary-age children develop basic learning skills through training in concentration.

Procedure: Most of the activities described in Section III, particularly those in Chapters 13 and 14, are excellent for helping children learn to concentrate. These exercises require children to focus their energy and attention and to discipline their minds.

Some of these activities may be a bit too complex or demanding for primary-age children. To begin to teach concentration to young children, short, simple exercises in focusing are appropriate. As they develop their abilities and become familiar with the idea of concentrating, even very young children can gradually develop more sustained concentration skills. An additional benefit of such activities is that they have a calming effect and can provide an excellent transition from one task to another.

Step 1: To begin, simply have the children, keeping their eyes closed, spend five minutes several times a day being completely quiet and still at their desks. Ideally, this step should be done before you begin work in the morning and before going from one activity to another. Concentration skills can only be developed within a quiet and calm atmosphere. Disruptions from the outside or noisy, restless children could disturb the equilibrium of the group and distract at least some of the children. As you develop your own energy awareness, you will become aware of subtle changes in energy in your students, which can provide valuable clues to how to interact with or guide the group.

Step 2: After at least a week of these short quiet times, begin playing soft, calming, flowing music during the sessions. Again, insist that everyone be quiet and still and keep their eyes closed; invite them to fill themselves completely with the music, tuning out everything else, including thoughts, body sensations, and other noises. Instruct them simply to refocus their attention to the music if they drift away and find themselves paying attention to other things. Continue having frequent daily sessions with music for at least a week.

Step 3: Find a large object or several smaller objects that have lights, are an interesting shape, or combine colors in an interesting way. (Many such knick-knacks are currently available in stores.) A large aquarium with several fish and plants, or something as simple as a candle, could be used. If the object is not large enough for the entire class to see easily, then you will have to divide into groups and use several objects. If possible, have the children sit in a circle. Tell them to focus all their attention on this object, entering it or becoming a part of it. Again, insist that everyone be still and quiet. If their attention drifts, instruct them to refocus. Do this step for a few minutes twice a day for a week or two, using different objects of visual interest if possible.

Step 4: Ask the children to talk about how they have experienced these concentration sessions. Do they feel differently before and after them? How has the group as a whole been affected by the exercises? Have the children noticed that it is easier for them to do their class work after these sessions?

To the Teacher: These activities will help children develop auditory and visual concentration as well as meditative skills. You are encouraged to adapt the exercise to the age, maturity, and development of your students and to build on this simple beginning.

These exercises can be integrated directly into the skills you are teaching by having the children talk, dictate sentences or stories, write, or draw pictures about their experiences. You can also use these exercises exclusively to build concentration, following each session with learning skills.

Be sensitive to the needs, moods, attitudes and energy level of the children. If the group has become "hyper," you should probably give them an opportunity to do some physical activities, then calming them down with a session in concentration.

TEACHING SCIENCE IN THE INTERMEDIATE GRADES BY USING THOUGHT-IMAGERY

Thoughts and images are a form of energy that we can deliberately focus on and channel with practice. In some instances, observable, predictable effects can be produced.

The following activity is fun, interesting, and different from many science experiments. It can also be used to teach children how to form and test hypotheses, observe and record data, set up a control, control variables, and identify uncontrolled variables.

Purpose: To have intermediate-grade students design and conduct an experiment in plant growth by using thought-imagery.

Procedure:

Step 1: Select three small plants or seedlings of similar development, or have students plant and grow them from seeds.

Step 2: Explain that the purpose of this experiment is to observe the effects of channeling positive thought-imagery, negative thought-imagery, and no thought-imagery on the growth and health of three plants.

Step 3: Explain the concept of energy fields, the notion that thought is a form of energy, and the concept of channeling energy (refer to Chapter 14). Explain that as a class, you will channel positive loving thoughts and visual images of a healthy, full plant to one plant, negative thoughts and images of poor growth to another plant, and no thoughts or images to the third plant.

Step 4: Teach them the experimental design you choose to use. Instruct them in identifying controlled and uncontrolled variables, the formulation of hypotheses, and recording data. All three plants must be raised and cared for in terms of watering and exposure to light in as similar a manner as possible.

Step 5: Conduct the experiment.

To the Teacher: You may wish to conduct this experiment with only two plants, channeling positive thought-imagery to one and none to the other, although the results may not be as dramatic. Much research has recently been published about the awareness and communication of plants, which would be interesting to your students and would help explain the results of this experiment. Plants also respond differently to various kinds of music, seeming to prefer the soft, classical kind to loud, jarring music like rock. You could incorporate music into your design.

Many other interesting experiments can be designed around the effects or function of different kinds of energy and such things as pyramid power.

TEACHING WRESTLING IN JUNIOR HIGH SCHOOL
BY USING ENERGY AWARENESS

There has been recent interest in mind-body approaches to sports and physical education. Many of these approaches borrow non-Western philosophies and techniques. Leonard (1977) indicated that many schools are beginning to offer new sports options like Tai Chi Chuan, body conditioning, yoga, and rock climbing. This broadening is part of a coming revolution in sports and physical education, sometimes called the New Physical Education. Certainly there was room for reform in traditional physical education, with its emphasis on dress codes, hair length, and competitive team sports. The shape this new mind-body approach will eventually take is still too early to tell. As an example we will take a traditional team sport such as wrestling and apply some of the new concepts to it.

Of all the traditional competitive contact sports, wrestling can make the best use of principles of energy awareness. Wrestlers often have to shift their center of gravity and change the direction of their energy rather quickly. Energy awareness incorporates other transpersonal communication skills such as centering, breathing, relaxation and concentration.

CHANGING YOUR CENTER OF GRAVITY

One of the most useful applications of energy awareness is to teach wrestlers how to raise or lower their center of gravity, depending on whether they need to have a heavy and low center or a light and high one.

Purpose: To teach wrestling skills to junior high school students by using activities in energy awareness.

Procedure:

Step 1: Ask your students to select a partner about their same size and weight so they can take turns lifting each other off the floor. Taking turns, each person lifts his partner by standing behind him and wrapping his arms around his partner's waist.

Step 2: First follow Step 1 by just having partners stand normally to determine how much energy it takes to lift them normally.

Step 3: Now ask each person being lifted to concentrate on being centered and sending his energy downward in his body through his legs and out the bottom of his feet, rooting him into the ground. It sometimes helps to have them imagine themselves with roots growing out of the bottom of their feet and spreading out under the ground. They continue to drain energy out of the upper body until all its weight seems to be resting on the bowl formed by the pelvis. Tell the students that when they are ready, they should signal their partners who will lift them as before. Caution those who are lifting not to suddenly jerk upward because it may break the concentration of a beginner. This lift will usually require a noticable increase in energy to even budge the other person.

Step 4: Now ask them to reverse their energy, this time sending it upward out the top of their heads. Ask them to imagine themselves being light and airy, with their energy lifting them upward. This time, lifting their partners is much easier.

Step 5: Discuss the differences the students noticed and how to use this skill in various aspects of wrestling, such as avoiding take-downs.

When they understand the concept, have them practice it in combination with various moves.

To the Teacher or Coach: There is no way to explain this concept completely except that we apparently can learn to exercise some control over our center of gravity through our thoughts. Energy is always moving in our bodies and it can be brought under conscious control. It is clear that there is a connection between thoughts and energy. The higher the quality of your thoughts, the higher the quality of your energy and strength.

THE RELAXED BODY

There has been an emphasis on strength coming from a tense, tight body, but recently we are beginning to understand the strength that comes from a relaxed body. The former has some definite limitations; energy can be concentrated in various muscle groups but not flow freely throughout the body. The relaxed athlete has much more flexibility and mobility. The following activity clearly demonstrates the strength of relaxed muscles over tense ones.

Purpose: To teach junior high school wrestlers the power of a relaxed body by using activities in energy awareness.

Procedure:

Step 1: Have your students select a partner about the same height and weight. While facing each other, each one takes a turn at making a tight fist and placing his tensed arm on the shoulder of his partner. Partners then try to bend the arm downward at the elbow. It may take considerable energy, but usually the arm will bend.

Step 2: Now have the students relax their arms and open their hands, laying their arms on their partners' shoulders. Ask them to relax their shoulders and arm, imagining that the arm is a beam of energy that stretches out from their shoulders and extends as far as they can imagine. Tell them to imagine this beam as straight and unbending, extending out to the ends of the universe. Tell them to focus their attention on "seeing" the energy extend from their finger tips and to continue to concentrate on this image as their partners try to bend their arms. As long as they maintain their focused concentration, it is almost impossible for their partners to bend their relaxed arms. Again ask partners to use gradually more pressure instead of a quick jerk of the arm, which would break the concentration of a beginner.

Step 3: This activity will amaze most people, and many will think there must have been some trick involved. Discuss the principle of *intention* with them; that is, the ability to focus on being relaxed and on the energy beam freed them from many of the constraints of our ordinary perception. This reaction often happens accidently to an athlete in either a stressful or ordinary situation. The experience has been described in various ways, with most athletes reporting a slowing down of time and an unreal detached feeling. These are moments when mind, body, and spirit are suddenly all in harmony.

To the Coach or Teacher: Discuss the application of these principles to wrestling, including the role of centering and breathing. Learning to look at the world with soft, partially closed eyes instead of hard, wide-open eyes is another important part of this harmony. The main application is to help your students learn that they can do what they need to do, on and off the mats, by relaxing, being centered, and having quiet, high-quality thoughts and intentions. If you can teach that concept with this activity, then you have accomplished more than just an improvement in wrestling ability.

TEACHING HISTORY IN HIGH SCHOOL
BY KEEPING A JOURNAL

One of the common complaints of students about history is that it often doesn't have any personal relevance to their present lives. This complaint is often justified because of the ways in which history is taught. The use of journal-keeping techniques is one way you as a teacher can begin to make history personally relevant and meaningful to your students.

In general, a transpersonal communications approach to history would involve a search for common experiences and threads that relate to students' present personal experiences. The so-called collective consciousness that has been present throughout history provides a rich source of these awarenesses.

Purpose: To teach high school students Revolutionary War concepts as part of American history by keeping a journal.

Procedure: As you start your unit on the Revolutionary War, your students begin to keep a daily journal. Teach them how to do so by using the journal-keeping activities in Chapter 17.

For each event, such as major battles or important gatherings like the writing and signing of the Declaration of Independence, ask your students to place themselves there at that scene as it was happening. Ask them to write about their impressions, thoughts, and feelings as someone who actually was at each of these historical events. Encourage them to write their impressions in their journals as if they occurred that same day. For example, an entry might include, "Today we debated about how King George might receive our grievances, and I said that we should not let our fears of George's reaction change our thinking. I hate to admit it, but I too often do let my fear of the reactions of others change my thinking."

You can augment this process by reading actual sections from various autobiographies of people who lived during this period of history. The autobiography of Benjamin Franklin would be helpful in this unit. Sometimes a biographer also captured the essence of an historical event in the subject's various personal reactions.

JOURNAL OF DIALOGUE

The journal of dialogue enables students to establish meaningful dialogue with any historical characters and events. Below is an illustration.

Purpose: To enable high school history students to have deep, meaningful dialogues with significant historical persons of the Revolutionary War period of American history by using journal-keeping techniques.

Procedure:

Step 1: After you have presented some material on various people who played an important role during the Revolution, ask your students to compile a list of persons with whom they would like to carry on a dialogue.

Step 2: Then ask them to write why they would wish to talk with this person. Ask them to identify the potential significance of the dialogue in their life today. You may wish to use this idea as an initial writing assignment.

Step 3: Ask them to chose one of the persons with whom to actually talk. Have them close their eyes and imagine that they are actually talking to this person. Ask them to imagine sitting in a room and the person walks in and sits in a facing chair. Have them feel, see, and hear the person's presence.

Step 4: Tell your students to begin an internal dialogue with this person by telling him or her why they wanted to talk to him or her. Have them tell the historical person what significance he or she has to them in their present life.

Step 5: Tell them to write both what they said and what replies they got. Have them record everything, whether it seems casual or profound. Tell them not to direct the dialogue completely, to let it take its own path. They speak, the historical person speaks, and the topics flow. Ask them to stay open to their transpersonal core and contact this person at that level. Only by keeping a quiet, attentive mind open to receiving can they actually enable the dialogue to reach this level.

Step 6: After they have completed their dialogue ask them to reread it and record any additional thoughts, feelings, and impressions. Have them focus on what meaning the dialogue has for them in their present circumstances. You also may ask them to read the dialogue aloud into a tape recorder and play it back, recording additional impressions.

To the Teacher: During these dialogues there may be pauses when your students are reflecting and gathering new energy. When they start again they may move to a deeper level of contact. Also, they may need to be encouraged to use several visits to deepen the contact.

IV

HOLISTIC PERSPECTIVES IN EDUCATION

20

The Transpersonal Teacher

Of all the teachers you have had, which ones stand out in your mind as the best? What qualities did you admire in them? Your list may differ some from others', but generally we will include personal qualities: "he had a sense of humor," "she took a personal interest in me," "he seemed to understand me," "she was 'real,'" "he never put me or anyone like me down for making a mistake," and so on.

Jackson (1968) estimated that elementary school teachers engage in over 1,000 daily exchanges with students. How teachers respond in these exchanges determines whether or not they are remembered as good teachers or not remembered at all. Teaching in the most complete sense is a process of communication.

Those personal qualities you recalled were probably as evident outside the classroom as within. This fact isn't unusual if you place any credence in the statement attributed to James Coleman: "The average adolescent is really in school, academically, for about ten minutes a day." Unfortunately, much of what is considered important or relevant to many children is not part of the formal curriculum and is relegated to a secondary role in the informal curriculum. The latter contains the important learning excluded from the regular curriculum because it is too real, controversial, or because it interferes with what is supposed to be taught.

Many studies have shown that teachers often have a limited awareness of the communication process involved in teaching. Martin and Keller (1974) found that teachers were unaware of such things as (1) the extent to which they call on boys or girls, (2) the frequency with which students approach them, (3) the number of times they initiate private contacts with students, and (4) the amount of class time they spend on routine or procedural matters.

Carkhuff (1974) noted that most children complete their entire education without a teacher or counselor ever responding once to the child's frame of reference, even though most of them would agree that there is where learning begins.

Carkhuff analyzed thousands of hours of classroom interactions without ever hearing a feeling word or a response to an expressed feeling that would indicate it was accurately understood.

Weinstein and Fantani (1970) concluded after a four-year search for effective teaching methods that much of the learning process itself should focus on helping children with their concerns.

COMMON MYTHS ABOUT TEACHING

It is very easy to adopt certain beliefs about what a teacher should be like or must be like. Most teachers have a set of beliefs about themselves in that role. These beliefs are often based upon some idealized image of what makes a good teacher, and they usually require the person to rise above her or his humanness. In addition, such beliefs serve as a form of protection against being real. The prospect of dropping their façades is often frightening to teachers who are not sure they will be liked or respected if students really know them. The following self-inventory may help you determine if you are still operating from any mistaken role expectations that could interfere with your effectiveness.

SELF-SURVEY ON COMMON BELIEFS
ABOUT TEACHING EFFECTIVELY

Directions: Place a check mark in the column that best represents your belief.

	Strongly Agree	Agree	Disagree	Strongly Disagree
1. Effective teachers must know the answers to students questions.				
2. Effective teachers must support each other and present a united front to students regardless of personal feelings or values.				
3. Effective teachers must be consistent in their dealings with students.				
4. Effective teachers must provide a learning environment that is challenging, stimulating, and free, yet quiet and orderly at all times.				
5. Effective teachers must be calm, never lose their tempers, or show strong emotions.				
6. Effective teachers must hide their real feelings from their students.				
7. Effective teachers must avoid any biases or prejudices. They are neither racist nor sexist.				
8. Effective teachers must display some degree of acceptance for all students. They never play favorites.				

Scoring: All the above statements are myths. They all ask the teacher to rise above all human frailties and try to become something or someone that no one can be.

TEACHERS' ATTITUDES

Teachers also may have developed a number of attitudes about the learning process that interfere with their relationships with students. The following self-survey may help you determine if you still have any attitudes that could interfere in this way.

SELF-SURVEY ON TEACHER ATTITUDES

Directions: The following are various types of behavior in which a teacher may engage in relation to students. Read each item carefully and then put a check mark in one of the columns to indicate what you would do.

As a Teacher, I:	*Make a Great Effort to Do This*	*Tend to Do This*	*Tend to Avoid Doing This*	*Make a Great Effort Not to Do This*
1. Closely supervise my students in order to get better work from them.				
2. Set the goals and objectives for my students and sell them on the merits of my plans.				
3. Set up controls to assure that my students are getting their work done.				
4. Encourage my students to set their own goals and objectives.				
5. Make sure that my students' work is planned for them.				
6. Check with my students daily to see if they need any help.				
7. Step in as soon as their work indicates that they are slipping.				
8. Push my students to meet schedules if necessary.				

	Make a Great Effort to Do This	Tend to Do This	Tend to Avoid Doing This	Make a Great Effort Not to Do This
9. Have frequent meetings with my students to keep in touch with them.				
10. Allow students to make all important decisions about their learning.				

_____ + _____ + _____ + _____ = _____

Total
Score

Scoring Procedures: Each item is weighted 1, 2, 3, or 4. Certain items are keyed with the rightmost column ("Make a Great Effort Not to Do This"), weighted at 4, and others with the leftmost column ("Make a Great Effort to Do This"), weighted at 4. The following key shows you how to score each item:

Items scored 1, 2, 3, 4 (far left = 1 and far right = 4) include numbers 1, 2, 3, 5, 6, 7, and 8.

Items scored 4, 3, 2, 1 (far left = 4 and far right = 1) include numbers 4, 9, and 10.

Write the appropriate number in the column where you placed a check mark. Add all the numbers in each column and add the sums of each column to get a total score. Place your score on the continuum below and look at the interpretation that fits your category.

10	25	40

10–19 strong need to control the learning environment
20–29 willingness to give up some control over the learning environment
30–39 willingness to facilitate student control of the learning environment

BELIEFS OF EFFECTIVE TEACHERS

Teachers who wish to develop transpersonal communication skills in themselves and their students need to examine their beliefs and attitudes toward teaching and learning. A teacher, to be effective in fostering transpersonal communication in the classroom, must have faith in and commitment to the self-discovery process. This is a process in which the teacher is able to create a learning environment that helps students develop their own self-knowledge.

Teachers teach more by *who they are* than by what they know. They model what they believe, and they communicate their beliefs by what they do and say. This factor becomes one of the most important aspects of teaching transpersonal communication in the classroom, and these beliefs and attitudes become the framework for any communication skills that teachers may learn. Without certain attitudes, beliefs, and understandings about children, the skills that teachers learn will not produce more effective transpersonal communication in their students.

There has been some research on the beliefs and attitudes associated with effectiveness in teachers, for example, an extensive study by Combs *et al.* (1969). The authors examined the beliefs of teachers in five areas: (1) their subjects or areas of knowledge; (2) their ideas of what people are like; (3) themselves and their concepts of themselves; (4) their purposes—society's, their own, and those related to their work; and (5) their approaches to their work. The results of this study suggested that effective teachers held certain beliefs in common.

AREAS OF KNOWLEDGE

Combs *et al.* found that knowledge about subject area must be so personally meaningful to the teacher that it becomes a belief in itself. A teacher can *know* about individual differences in children, but if he doesn't *believe* it, he won't use it in his teaching. Teaching methods and the information related to them must have personal meaning in order to be incorporated.

WHAT PEOPLE ARE LIKE

Here clear differences were found between effective and ineffective teachers.

Able–Unable. Effective teachers perceive children as having the capacity to deal with their problems as opposed to doubting this capacity.

Friendly–Unfriendly. Effective teachers see children as being friendly and well intentioned. They do not regard children as threatening and evil.

Worthy–Unworthy. Effective teachers see children as being worthy rather than unworthy. They see them as having dignity and integrity which must be respected and maintained. They do not see children as unimportant beings whose dignity and integrity may be violated or discounted.

Internally–Externally Motivated. Effective teachers see children and their behavior as essentially coming from within rather than responding to external stimuli. They see children as creative and dynamic rather than passive or static, to be molded and directed.

Dependable–Undependable. Effective teachers see children as essentially trustworthy and dependable in the sense of behaving in predictable ways. They regard the behavior of children as understandable rather than capricious, unpredictable, or negative.

Helpful–Hindering. Effective teachers see children as being basically willing to help. They regard children as important sources of satisfaction rather than of frustration and suspicion.

WHAT I AM LIKE

Effective teachers know how to use *self* as an instrument. They are willing and able to share themselves and to deal appropriately with themselves and life.

Identified–Apart. Effective teachers feel identity with others rather than separateness. They see themselves as similar to others rather than removed, apart, or alienated.

197

Adequate–Inadequate. Effective teachers feel basically adequate rather than inadequate and capable of dealing with problems.

Trustworthy–Untrustworthy. Effective teachers see themselves as essentially dependable and reliable. Ineffective teachers tend to have doubts about themselves in these areas.

Wanted–Unwanted. Effective teachers see themselves as wanted rather than unwanted. They see themselves as essentially likeable, warm, attractive, and receiving responses in the same manner.

Worthy–Unworthy. Effective teachers see themselves as worthy rather than unworthy. They see themselves as persons of dignity and integrity and worthy of respect.

WHAT MY PURPOSES ARE

The effective teachers were found to have goals different from those of ineffective teachers. The purposes of the latter tend to inhibit their ability to teach.

Freeing–Controlling. Effective teachers see their purpose as that of freeing rather than of controlling people, of assisting, releasing, and facilitating rather than manipulating, coercing, blocking, or inhibiting behavior.

Larger–Smaller Issues. Effective teachers tend to be more concerned with large rather than small issues, and they have a broad rather than narrow perspective. They seem to have more long-ranged views rather than immediate and specific ones.

Self-Revealing–Self-Concealing. Effective teachers are more likely to be self-revealing than self-concealing. They can treat their feelings and shortcomings as important, and they can be open about them. They seem willing to be persons and not roles.

Involved–Alienated. Effective teachers tend to be involved with people rather than alienated from them. Their purpose is to interact with students instead of being inert or remaining aloof or remote.

Process Oriented–Goal Oriented. Effective teachers are more interested in processes than in achieving goals. They see their purpose as encouraging and facilitating the process of search and discovery as opposed to working toward some personal goal or preconceived solution.

APPROACHES TO THE TASK

Teachers' beliefs about how to approach the teaching–learning task were found to relate to their success.

People–Things. Effective teachers are more oriented toward people than things, toward students rather than subjects.

Subjective–Objective. Effective teachers are more likely to approach students subjectively and are more concerned with the experience of learning rather than objective facts.

TEACHERS' MISCONCEPTIONS ABOUT CHILDREN

Teachers often don't understand children because they see them as miniature adults. When children behave like children instead of like adults, often teachers feel angry, scared, and sad. Admittedly, it would be easier to teach if children looked at the world and behaved as adults do. However, they don't. Understanding how they look at the world and why they do and say what they do helps to build the rapport needed for effective teaching (Holt, 1974). Below are some characteristics teachers tend to overlook.

1. Children are concrete and not abstract. They may need concrete examples in order to understand concepts.
2. They seem happy and carefree because they use their energy and curiosity to discover new things and not to brood about old things.
3. Even though they seem happy and carefree they can have as many fears as most adults.
4. They are sensual. They are aware of their senses and respond to what their senses tell them. They often do what feels good at the moment.
5. They are self-absorbed and self-centered. They often don't naturally see things from another person's point of view, a quality that needs to be developed through interaction with other children.
6. They often appear cruel and inconsiderate. What adults fail to see is that whether they are cruel or kind depends upon an impulse rather than a plan or principle.

ELEMENTS OF EFFECTIVE
TEACHER-STUDENT RELATIONSHIPS

In order to build an effective relationship with students, a teacher must be able to see children as they are and not as he or she would like them to be. In addition, teachers and students need the following:

1. *Openness to each other:* a willingness to risk being open, direct, and honest with each other.
2. *Caring:* each must value the relationship and care what happens to the other.
3. *Interdependence* (as opposed to dependence): each must view his goals as characterized by interrelatedness.
4. *Separateness:* each must be willing to see the other as a separate person who will grow and develop in unique, creative, and individual ways.
5. *Mutual needs and wants:* neither person's needs and wants can be met at the expense of the other's.

2I

Teaching
as Transpersonal
Communication

THREE VIEWS OF THE ROLE OF THE TEACHER

There are three distinct views on the role of the teacher. The first emphasizes the teacher's role as a *transmitter of knowledge*. This view assumes that there exists a well-known and finite body of knowledge from which the teacher selects certain facts to pass on to the pupil. A further assumption is that students need basic facts and information before they can think for themselves. The problem with this approach is that the teacher usually ends up learning much more than the students.

The second view involves the teacher as a *guide* to student inquiry and discovery. The teacher asks questions that help the learner understand the structure of each discipline, so that even a young child can think like a historian or a scientist. The major problem with this approach is that it runs counter to some of the established research on child development. It assumes a cognitive level necessary to handle abstract concepts that is reached by probably less than 50 percent of adults.

The third view stresses the development of a warm human relationship between teacher and student. The key to learning is the creation of a healthy environment based on sincerity, honesty, and respect for each other's wants and needs. Where this model breaks down is that very few teachers know how to create and maintain that kind of climate in the classroom. When they try and fail they often become cynical and rejecting in their communication with others.

Toffler (1970) indicates some new directions for education that have implications for the teacher's role. He suggests that in order to teach people how to cope with future shock, teachers must reduce their attention to facts and information and instead focus more on the process of learning; such learning may require the elimination of a substantial part of the formal curriculum in favor of a more mobile one designed to increase the individual's ability to cope with change. Toffler strongly suggests that all students should be taught certain common skills needed for communication and social integration. The teacher in this design becomes more important than ever in teaching communication processes such as how to learn, relearn, and unlearn if necessary; to make choices from an internal system of values; and to relate effectively to others.

Most teachers don't pay attention to these aspects of teaching because they don't know how to. Their training probably paid little attention to communication processes and skills such as these, and many teachers angrily blame their own teachers for not providing these skills.

Many in-service programs have tried to help teachers learn communication skills with some promising results. A research study by Aspy (1969) showed that following an in-service program directed at teaching these skills to teachers, there were increases of ten or more points in their students I.Q.'s. Further research by Aspy and Roebuck (1976) showed that there were discrepencies of two years or more between the achievement levels of students who had teachers with good communication skills as opposed to those who did not. They concluded that the level of communication skills determined whether the contact these teachers had with students facilitated or retarded the learning process. This research clearly indicates the importance of good communication skills in the learning process and the possibility of remediation for teachers with poor communication skills.

Coleman *et al.* (1966) found in their massive study of educational opportunity that students who felt good about themselves were successful in school. Even more importantly, they found that this feeling of personal efficacy was more important in predicting success in school than any of the other factors examined, including social class, race, pupil-teacher ratios, number of books in the school library, and the educational background of the teachers.

TRANSPERSONAL VERSUS HUMANISTIC EDUCATION

Transpersonal education grew out of the humanistic education movement. The distinctions can become blurred and may be unnecessary, but some similarities and differences are worth noting. Both transpersonal education and humanistic education emphasize the development of the emotional side of human behavior and a personal frame of reference. One of the major differences seems to be in the emphasis placed upon ego processes.

Humanistic education and communication emphasize strong ego development based upon authentic personal expression and internal values. On the other hand, transpersonal approaches tend to emphasize transcending the ego so that unity with the universe can be achieved.

Humanistic education also seems to focus on the interpersonal aspects of behavior, whereas transpersonal education focuses on intrapersonal experiences which connect the individual with universal energy and inner serenity. Transpersonal education is somewhat less likely to be tied to past experience or social convention than are humanistic approaches.

Because of the emphasis on ego processes, humanistic education aims for high levels of self-esteem, love, belonging, and social esteem, whereas transpersonal education is more interested in helping people transcend the self and achieve mastery over the ego by assuming the power and responsibility to create their own life experiences.

Finally, humanistic education traditionally has focused on improving self-concept, and transpersonal education emphasizes the mastery or surrender of personal desires. It is our contention that this mastery is not possible unless people already have healthy self-concepts.

Abraham Maslow, one of the founders of the humanistic education movement, also was the first to announce the new transpersonal approach. He wrote in the preface to his second edition of *Toward a Psychology of Being:* "I should say also that I consider Humanistic, Third Force Psychology to be transitional, a preparation for still higher Fourth

Psychology, transpersonal, transhuman, centered in the cosmos rather than in human needs and interest, going beyond humanness, identity, self-actualization and the like."[1]

Maslow's prediction certainly has come true, and in many areas, transpersonal education is extending what has been developed as part of humanistic education. All methods and materials developed in humanistic education can be used in the search for a more complete system of human functioning.

EDUCATING THE LOWER AND HIGHER SELF

Despite some advances in open school architecture, most children who enter school still are faced with the standard classroom: one teacher facing fixed rows of students who are asked to jump through academic hoops that have little meaning to either them or their teacher. They are taught by this system to adapt to a hierarchical structure much like what they will find in the industrial factory. One alert ninth-grade student said, "I mostly go to school to be with my friends; the rest of what goes on in school is their trip [the school officials]."

In addition, we may have used our schools as an instrument of social control to systematically eliminate any form of natural expression from our children. One student related that in her school the students aren't even allowed to run at recess time. Our schools are not places where children can find support and nurturing for their natural feelings of joy, sadness, anger, fear, and excitement. Instead, many schools have become rigid, joyless, repressive structures devoid of any feelings. The main objective of the majority of teachers still is to prepare children to find work that even the teachers find boring, meaningless, and oppressive.

One thing missing in all of this, is education directed toward teaching children to have a fuller appreciation of their lower and higher selves. You may ask: What are the lower and higher selves? How can we teach what we don't know?

[1]Abraham Maslow, *Toward a Psychology of Being* (New York: Van Nostrand, 1968), p. 4.

THE LOWER SELF

The lower self has been described in many ways, but primarily it contains our connection to other forms of life, such as plants and animals. It contains our genetic survival mechanisms, like the adrenal stress reaction, which produces "freeze, fight, or flight" reactions automatically as a response to perceived danger. The lower self contains all our basic feelings, fundamental drives, and primitive urges. It contains evolutionary puddles of energy attached to pair-bonding, territorial imperatives and other basic human processes. Full communication with and acceptance of this lower self is an essential part of grounding, centering, and learning.

Schools have traditionally attempted to eliminate many aspects of the lower self, considering them counterproductive in the learning process. We all have had to fight against this form of oppression in order to preserve or restore our naturalness and humanness.

It is clear that many of us have been taught to place shackles on our lower or natural selves. This process has denied our history, and worse, denied the most natural and spontaneous parts of our selves.

When Don Juan decided to teach Carlos Castaneda how to become a "man of knowledge," he began by educating the lower self. He helped Carlos to discover his "tonals," or connections with other animals. One such session involved Carlos taking peyote until he reached a level of consciousness where he became like a dog. He said,

> I looked at the dog and his mane was like mine. We played and wrestled until I knew his wishes and he knew mine. We took turns manipulating each other in the fashion of a puppet show. I could make him move his legs by twisting my toes, and every time he nodded his head I felt an irresistible impulse to jump. But his most impish act was to make me scratch my head with my foot while I sat, he did it by flapping his ears from side to side. This action was to me utterly, unbearably funny. Such a touch of grace and irony; such mastery. . . .

Slowly Carlos integrated his experience: ". . . The awakening to serious, sober consciousness was genuinely shocking. I had forgotten I was a man!"[2]

[2]Carlos Castaneda, *The Teachings of Don Juan* (New York: Ballantine Books, 1968), p. 34.

THE HIGHER SELF

The expansion of consciousness must include our connections with other life forms as part of our basic human nature. A denial of this unmistakable fact has been a serious oversight in the study of human consciousness, which tends to restrict its focus to higher forms. The Self, with a capital "S," refers to what Assagioli (1965) termed the higher self. Jung's definition of the Self was the center of psychic awareness which transcends ego awareness and includes those aspects of the psyche that are part of the unconscious. Jung (1938) believed that by descending through the depths of your own psyche, you would experience the deepest layer of transpersonal communication, where the true meaning of life resides. It would be more accurate, according to this conception, to call the Self the deepest self, which would include the higher and lower self.

In the context of transpersonal communication, the higher self represents those aspects of the self that transcend the individuality or uniqueness of the individual and enable us to experience a deep connection with all other Selves, for example, the experience of unconditional love. Traditionally, the education of the higher self has been left to the realm of theology. However, we are now seeing more clearly that education of the higher self is a legitimate goal of any institution involved in education.

Transpersonal communication seeks to provide a framework for the study and development of higher and lower states of.consciousness, including our natural and spiritual realms as essential parts of human life. The higher and lower selves are seen as part of our transpersonal core, where we experience our union with all life energy.

THE HISTORY OF COMMUNICATIONS IN EDUCATION

Any study of the role of communications in education has to begin with the work of John Dewey. He challenged the prevailing philosophies, which viewed the child as an empty vessel awaiting patiently and quietly to be filled up with knowledge. Dewey believed education was a carefully guided experience for children, arranged according to their interests and capacities. He required teachers to know each student as a person. Unfortunately, when many of Dewey's ideas were put into practice, in the progressive movement, they bore little resemblance to the original precepts.

Actually, Dewey's theories were better understood and practiced in England, where educators began to see that the relationship between the teacher and learner was the crucial variable in the learning process. Dewey's philosophies were combined with the theories and techniques of Piaget in the development of the English informal infant and primary schools. While this was happening in English schools, a far different movement was sweeping through American ones.

SPUTNIK AND SCHOOL COUNSELING

We went through a period of American education where the ideas of strong classicists and scientists like Robert Hutchins, James Conant, and Admiral Rickover prevailed. The launching of Sputnik by the Russians in 1957 was all the ammunition many critics needed to call for an even tougher scientific, cognitively oriented curriculum. Interestingly, this event also marked the beginning of the school guidance counseling movement. The National Defense Education Act set up training institutes to provide more counselors, whose task was to "counsel" more students into the sciences. The school guidance movement also held some promise for helping to humanize or personalize learning through individual and small-group counseling. However, school counselors with 500 to 800 pupil case loads found themselves too often handling crises and routine administrative functions, such as filling out recommendations and processing college applications. Needless to say, the efforts of counselors have not affected the mainstream of the school or its curriculum. The scientific reform movement existed from about 1955 to 1965, and when the dust had settled, very little had changed in the nature of the teacher-student relationship or the methods of teaching. John Goodlad reported in a study of this reform movement released in 1969 that "Teaching was predominantly telling and questioning by the teacher with children responding one by one or occasionally in chorus."[3]

[3]John Goodlad, "The Schools vs. Education," *Saturday Review* (April 19, 1969), p. 82.

THIRD-FORCE PSYCHOLOGY AND
HUMANISTIC EDUCATION

The person most responsible for bringing humanistic psychology to the schools was Carl Rogers. In his book *Freedom To Learn*, he wrote, ". . . the facilitation of significant learning rests upon certain attitudinal qualities which exist in the personal relationship between the facilitator and the learner."[4] Rogers and his associates had discovered the effectiveness of this principle in psychotherapy and found that it applied to classroom learning equally well. He further states, "When a facilitator creates, even to a modest degree, a classroom climate characterized by all that he can achieve of realness, prizing and empathy; when he trusts the constructive tendency of the individual and the group then he discovers that he has inaugurated an educational revolution."[5]

Many other humanistic educators have drawn on these principles in their research and have found that indeed the quality of the relationship between teacher and student is a vital part of learning. Good, *et al.* (1975), after reviewing studies on the effects of teachers' communication on learning, concluded that the level of empathic understanding in teachers was directly related to gains in academic achievement in their students.

A study by Newburg and Borton (1971) investigated the effects of a program emphasizing affective communication on academic achievement and reading skills. They found no differences in achievement test scores or in reading comprehension between treatment and control classes and concluded that ". . . affective students learn as much as controls in reading comprehension and history knowledge and also gain more positive attitudes towards themselves and teachers and a knowledge and use of various personal and interpersonal processes."[6]

Another interesting attempt to humanize the curriculum developed out of a Ford Foundation–Esalen Institute joint project led by George I. Brown. He and his staff developed "confluent education" as an integration of affective and cognitive learning. They began to redesign the traditional curriculum to enable both elements to merge equally. Students who were

[4]Carl Rogers, *Freedom To Learn* (Columbus, Ohio: Charles F. Merrill Books, 1969), p. 42.

[5]*Ibid.*, p. 43.

[6]Norman Newberg and Terry Borton, in ed. W. Gollub, *Effective Education Development Program Research Report*, Philadelphia School District, 1971, p. 98.

exposed to a confluent educational curriculum achieved better learning of cognitive materials; heightened motivation and response to learning; greater appreciation of self, nature, others, feelings, etc.; increased sense of responsibility; lessened desire for drugs or other forms of escape (Brown, 1971).

PSYCHOLOGICAL EDUCATION:
A CURRICULUM FOR PERSONAL EDUCATION

Many of the humanistic and affective education programs began to see that children could easily learn the communication skills they were teaching to teachers. Psychological education seeks to promote healthy personal growth as part of the regular curriculum. It's goal is to design curriculum units that have direct psychological impact on all students. Many such programs had high school students learning interpersonal communication skills and then assuming some role where they used the skills, such as teaching in an elementary classroom, counseling peers, or working in a nursery school.

Early evidence on the possible gains from this kind of program showed that pupils in these classes were seen by others as having achieved higher levels of psychological maturity than comparable pupils in regular classes; were less stereotyped in their thinking; were rated higher on measured levels of moral maturity; and indicated that they felt more mature, at ease with adults, better able to communicate, and more self-confident than before taking the course (Sprinthall and Sprinthall, 1974).

Other well-known programs, like the Human Development Program (HDP), have developed a structured small-group activity extending from preschool through high school. Through the use of "Magic Circle" groups, the children are taught skills in awareness, self-confidence, and social interaction. The activities are presented in weekly units that include each of these areas. Although the HDP does not intend to increase academic skills, many experimental studies have shown significant gains in I.Q. and such skills as vocabulary and reading for students having regular HDP groups. One of the key problems with so-called "canned" programs like HDP is the skill level of the teacher. Some programs offer training, whereas others merely rely on detailed instructions for the teacher. In either case, there is no guarantee a trained, sensitive teacher will be using these materials.

TRANSPERSONAL COMMUNICATION IN EDUCATION

At this time there are no transpersonal communication programs comparable to HDP, but several books published recently have contained some basic transpersonal communication exercises (Hendricks and Wills, 1975; Hendricks and Fadiman, 1976; Hendricks and Roberts, 1977).

A recent article by Samples (1977) presents a new model of learning that holds some promise of providing a more transpersonal basis for communication. His conception emphasizes a merger of left and right brain functions. The most current theory about the function of the brain halves is that the left brain directs rational linear thinking. It produces the structure and order present in reading, writing, and arithmetic. By contrast, the right brain controls metaphoric thinking, which is analogic, intuitive, and holistic. Samples has been able to develop curriculum materials that bring both left and right brain functions into partnership. His preliminary evaluations have shown that this development results in "(1) higher feelings of self-confidence, self-esteem and compassion, (2) wider exploration of traditional content, subjects and skills, and (3) higher levels of creative invention in content and skills."[7]

According to Samples, "The metaphoric mind presumes connectedness and searches it out. The rational mind presumes separateness and creates."[8] Watts (1968) states that the favorite mind game of Western thinkers is dividing whole experiences into parts and then tangling themselves up trying to decide which parts of the experience are causes and which are effect.

Transpersonal communication uses metaphoric thinking in centering, concentration, imagery, and dreams. All of these involve cyclical rather than linear thought. Concepts such as birth and death also take on new meaning when taken out of the usual linear mode. The first new under-

[7]Robert Samples, "Mind Cycles and Learning," *Phi Delta Kappan* (May 1977), pp. 688–92.

[8]*Ibid.*, p. 43.

standing to emerge is that birth and death are cycles that persons experience many times; only the physical forms have been discovered and categorized as the events, thereby marking the beginning and ending of our postnatal lives. The other understanding that emerges is the unity we have with other living things. For example, what connections do we have with trees which lose their leaves every fall and then produce new ones in the spring? Transpersonal communication can begin to open many new doors for discovering our connectedness and relatedness to each other and to the world around us. At this basic level, we are all alienated from ourselves, our natural selves, which include the lower and higher selves. The metaphoric mind is the source of many transpersonal communication skills, and as we learn these skills, we can begin to restore our sense of natural unity with ourselves, other people, and the world we live in.

THE TRANSPERSONAL SCHOOL

Holt (1972) tells of being propelled into the future to an imaginary society. After being shown where people live, work, and play he asks:

> "But where are your schools?"
> "Schools? What are schools?" is the reply.
> "Schools are places where people go to learn things."
> "I do not understand," he says, "people learn things everywhere, in all places."[9]

The transpersonal school is one that ideally exists everywhere, where learning is integrated with life. Obviously, this has not been our tradition, and so the ideal of the transpersonal school remains just that, an idea. In the meantime, it is possible to transform American education within its existing structure. This book is not a utopian treatise that outlines some vague, abstract "school-in-the-sky" concepts. It is a practical how-to-do-it guide to help teachers, counselors, and administrators learn skills, communication skills, necessary for survival within schools as they now exist.

[9]John Holt, *Freedom and Beyond* (New York: Dell Publishing Co., 1972), p. 117.

The underlying theory in this book is communications theory, and its application is a communications approach to teaching. In that approach the quality of the relationship between teacher and student is the key concept. Essential to the effectiveness is a teacher who knows himself or herself quite well, a teacher who is able to communicate with him- or herself, other people, and in a broader sense with that which is transpersonal.

In addition, this book emphasizes process rather than goal-oriented learning. That is, learning and using communication skills is a process and not a goal. We believe the processes in this book are essential for survival of the species.

What this book is *not* is one that provides answers to all school problems. We honestly don't know how to motivate someone to learn within a curriculum that to him or her is irrelevant and boring. We don't know how to get rid of bad teachers or how to make parents take more interest in schools or a myriad of other problems. What we do know is that teachers know a great deal about how to teach, but they just don't seem to have many opportunities to do it anymore. We think that the skills in this book could help; they could help teachers, counselors, administrators, and parents be more successful at doing what they know how to do.

V

A PARENT'S GUIDE TO TRANSPERSONAL COMMUNICATION

22

Transpersonal
Communication
at Home

PARENT'S ROLE

This book has been written primarily to help teachers and counselors integrate communication skills into the school. Teachers have direct and daily contact with their students. This relationship between teacher and student, although it usually takes place in a group, often lasts for hours each day. This school seems to us to be an ideal place for both teacher and student to learn more effective communication skills.

We also see potential in parents and children using this book to learn these skills. It will not only strengthen the efforts of the teachers and counselors, but more importantly, parents can learn from their children. In this society we have not examined the potential of children teaching parents, but the rapid changes in values and information have made this process almost a necessity. Many parents, scared and confused by these changes, often act in rejecting ways toward their children. This reaction can become aggravated when their children become teenagers and have more power themselves. When parents find that the power they once had over their children is diminished, they become even more frightened.

Our obvious alternative to that ineffective way of dealing with the realities of change is to find a common frame of reference for talking about fears, values, and problems. This book could begin to provide that frame of reference, and most of the activities can be easily adapted for use by parents and their children.

This kind of learning can be exciting and can lead to a rich supportive relationship between parent and children without all the power plays and rebellion that often characterize family communication. Maybe for the first time your children can get to know you as a person and not just as a parent, and you can begin to appreciate your children as people instead of some stereotyped image.

TIPS FOR PARENTS

REMOVE THE BLOCKS

One of the first blocks you may have to overcome is thinking that you are not smart enough or educated enough to use these activities. The truth is, any parent can use them. You don't have to be a college graduate or a psychiatrist or anything special to do the activities with your children. You do have to be able to read, of course, and use reasonable judgment and maturity. It also helps if you are open to change, open to learning new concepts, fairly flexible, and have a good sense of humor. If you care about improving and strengthening the relationship with your children you will find plenty of support and help from this book.

DEVELOP A COMFORTABLE STYLE

Not all learning of this kind is fun because it sometimes means changing cherished beliefs, attitudes, and behaviors. Certainly, if you do decide to use the book as a means for growth and change, you will enrich your life and probably your children's lives as well.

Be as natural and relaxed with the activities as possible. Don't push your children to participate if they are not interested. You can use the activities with your spouse or do many of them yourself. Ask your children to select activities they would like to do with you instead of prescribing for them.

TIMING IS IMPORTANT

Most of these activities do not require a lot of time. However, it is best to set aside a certain time rather than waiting until there is nothing else to do. Ask everyone to make a commitment to a certain amount of time. There are some times that are more conducive than others. Trips in the car usually offer opportunities to talk and use some of the activities. Meal times, when the family is together, can also be a time for learning and sharing. Also problems or discussions may come up that are natural times to use certain activities. It is best, for example, to have a real problem when practicing problem-solving skills.

EXAMINE YOUR EXPECTATIONS

What you can expect from these activities is a lot of honest introspection and some slow changes in beliefs, attitudes, values, and behaviors. You can expect to get to know yourself and your children more fully and completely.

What you can't expect are overnight changes in your behavior or the behavior of your children. It took a long time to develop the attitudes and behaviors you currently have, and it will take a while for noticeable changes.

QUESTIONS PARENTS OFTEN ASK ABOUT TRANSPERSONAL COMMUNICATION

1. *How is transpersonal communication going to help me with discipline?*

Transpersonal communication helps create a new framework for discipline based upon mutual respect. Realistic and necessary rules are established cooperatively and consequences are developed with mutual agreement. Unnecessary rules are also eliminated cooperatively. Necessary rules would include not doing anything that interferes with another person's productivity nor destructive behavior directed at people or materials. Other rules are added by the group as the need arises.

2. *Much of these activities seem like play; how will transpersonal communication increase other skills needed to get along in the world?*

There is an old adage that most teachers know a lot about teaching but they just don't have many opportunities to do it; and most students know a lot about learning and they just don't have many opportunities to do it. What seems to block the teaching-learning process, in our opinion, is ineffective communication. When effective interpersonal, intrapersonal, and transpersonal communication is present all learning is accelerated. The quality of the relationship between teacher and student is an important variable.

3. *Because of this emphasis, are children only going to do the things they want to do?*

Every child is expected to learn what is available to them to learn. One unmistakable fact is that we only learn what we want to learn. We sometimes mistake performing various mental activities for learning. Children learn all the time, and they learn those things that have relevance and importance to them. Because transpersonal communication can help them become more clear about what is relevant and important to them, it can increase their motivation to learn.

4. *How will this approach affect my child's performance on standardized tests?*

We know that standardized tests do not truly test a child's capacity, but they do seem to be important to society at this time. We still need to develop more comprehensive ways of measuring what children learn that include social, emotional, physical, and intuitive development, as well as intellectual development. Transpersonal communication can help sharpen a child's intellectual capacities because it helps remove blocks to memory and teaches effective concentration skills.

5. *Does "transpersonal" mean that my children are receiving religious training in school?*

Emphatically, no. Although some of the activities are derived from Eastern philosophies, they are not part of any religious discipline or dogma. For example, there is a clear distinction between Buddhist religious dogma and Buddhist philosophies. There is also confusion between the word "religious" and "spiritual." "Religious" means a set of beliefs and teachings about a supernatural being. "Spiritual" on the other hand relates to the highest qualities of the human mind or the soul of man.

23

Suggestions for Introducing Transpersonal Communication in Your School District

You, like many parents, may feel out of touch with what is really happening in your child's school. Also, you may be confused by the educational jargon that school officials tend to use.

What is true is that schools have changed and have improved in many ways. Some of the changes have been in the external appearance of schools, in audio-visual equipment, in laboratories, or in the curriculum. Where many schools have changed the least is in communications and human relations, the way people talk to and deal with each other. It is important to observe closely what patterns of communication and human relations exist in your child's school.

The following questions may help you evaluate whether your child's school needs more effective communications:

1. Do counselors actually counsel, or are they used as disciplinarians or program checkers?
2. How much one-to-one time do teachers have to spend with students who need it?
3. Is the school atmosphere relaxed and informal, or is it tense and formalized?
4. Do teachers or administrators use corporal punishment?

5. Are students able to participate in setting school and/or classroom rules?
6. Is there time in the curriculum for teachers to hold class discussion on student concerns?
7. Do teachers generally try to resolve their conflicts with students themselves, or do they send the student to the office?
8. When you go to school do you see signs of mutual respect and caring?
9. Is there evidence of student self-discipline, or do teachers have to use power (threats, ordering, yelling) to control students?
10. Do students have a say in what they are taught, at what rate, and how it will be evaluated?
11. Are students asked to evaluate their teachers to provide feedback to them?
12. Is a competitive grading system used to evaluate performance?
13. What is the student-to-teacher ratio in the classroom? Student-to-counselor ratio?
14. Are students bored and unhappy with school?

SUGGESTIONS ON INFORMAL EVALUATION

1. Make an appointment to meet with the principal, counselor and some of your child's teachers. Tell them you want to know more about them and the school, and ask them some of the questions listed above.
2. Visit several classes to determine the validity of their answers, and answer some of the questions for yourself.
3. Interview other students, and ask them some of the same questions.
4. Ask your child these questions too.
5. If you wish to introduce transpersonal communication, work through existing groups such as the P.T.A. or other advisory groups to the school.
6. You can also invite professionals who use this book to speak at a meeting of parents and teachers or to hold a workshop on this topic. If you write to the authors they will suggest possible people in your area who could speak at your school.

7. In introducing this material into a school, the key person is usually the principal. Get his or her suggestions. If you don't get any suggestions, you know you will have a tough job getting the material into the school.
8. You may find a receptive teacher or two who would be willing to begin using the activities. Work with them to develop a pilot program, if possible.

Bibliography

ASPY, DAVID. *Florida Journal of Educational Research II* (1969), pp. 39–48.

ASPY, DAVID, and FRANK ROEBUCK. *Affective Ingredients of a Human Education.* Amherst, Mass.: Human Resource Development Press, 1976.

ASSAGIOLI, ROBERTO. *Psychosynthesis.* New York: Viking Compass Book, 1965.

BABCOCK, DOROTHY E., and TERRY D. KEEPERS. *Raising Kids OK.* New York: Grove Press, 1976.

BALL, GERALDINE. *Magic Circle.* La Mesa, Cal.: Human Development Training Institute, Inc., 1974.

BROWN, GEORGE ISAAC. *Human Teaching for Human Learning.* New York: The Viking Press, 1971.

BROWN, GEORGE ISAAC, THOMAS YEOMANS, and LILES GRIZZARD, eds. *The Live Classroom.* New York: The Viking Press, 1975.

CANFIELD, JACK, and HAROLD C. WELLS. *100 Ways to Enhance Self-Concept in the Classroom.* Englewood Cliffs, N.J.: Prentice-Hall, Inc., 1976.

CARKHUFF, ROBERT R. *How to Help Yourself.* Amherst, Mass.: Human Resource Development Press, 1974.

CASTENADA, CARLOS. *The Teachings of Don Juan: A Yaqui Way of Knowledge.* New York: Ballantine Books, 1968.

CASTILLO, GLORIA A. *Left-Handed Teaching.* New York: Praeger Publishers, 1974.

CLARK, FRANCES VAUGHAN. "Rediscovering Transpersonal Education." *The Journal of Transpersonal Psychology*, 6, No. 1 (1974), 1–7.

COLEMAN, JAMES S., *et al. Equality of Educational Opportunity.* Washington, D.C.: U.S. Department of HEW, 1966.

COMBS, ARTHUR. *The Professional Education of Teachers.* Boston, Mass.: Allyn and Bacon, 1965.

COMBS, ARTHUR W., *et al. Florida Studies in the Helping Professions.* University of Florida Social Science Monograph No. 37. Gainsville: University of Florida Press, 1969.

DEROPP, ROBERT S. *The Master Game.* New York: Dell Publishing Co., 1968.

EPSTEIN, CHARLOTTE. *Affective Subjects in the Classroom: Exploring Race, Sex and Drugs.* Scranton, Pa.: Intext Educational Publishers, 1972.

FADIMAN, JAMES, and ROBERT FRAGER. *Personality and Personal Growth.* New York: Harper & Row, Publishers, 1976.

FEARN, LEIF. *Individual Development.* San Diego, Cal.: Education Improvement Associates, 1973.

FORMAN, ROBERT A., ed. *The Truth About Psychology.* San Francisco: Theta Seminars, 1976.

GOLDSTEIN, JOSEPH. *The Experience of Insight: A Natural Unfolding.* Santa Cruz, Cal.: Unity Press, 1976.

GOOD, THOMAS L., BRUCE J. BIDDLE, and JENE E. BROPHY. *Teachers Make a Difference.* New York: Holt, Rinehart and Winston, 1975.

GOODLAND, JOHN. "The Schools vs. Education." *Saturday Review* (April 19, 1969).

GORDON, THOMAS. *Teacher Effectiveness Training.* New York: David McKay Company, Inc., 1974.

GRINDER, JOHN, and RICHARD BANDLER. *The Structure of Magic, Vol. II.* Palo Alto, Cal.: Science and Behavior Books, Inc., 1976.

HARMEN, MERRILL, HOWARD KIRSCHENBAUM, and SIDNEY B. SIMON. *Clarifying Values Through Subject Matter.* Minneapolis, Minn.: Winston Press, Inc., 1973.

HENDRICKS, GAY, and JAMES FADIMAN. *Transpersonal Education.* Englewood Cliffs, N.J.: Prentice-Hall, Inc., 1976.

HENDRICKS, GAY, and RUSSEL WILLS. *The Centering Book.* Englewood Cliffs, N.J.: Prentice-Hall, Inc., 1975.

HENDRICKS, GAY, and THOMAS B. ROBERTS. *The Second Centering Book.* Englewood Cliffs, N.J.: Prentice-Hall, Inc., 1977.

HOLT, JOHN. *Freedom and Beyond.* New York: Dell Publishing Co., Inc., 1972.

———. *Escape From Childhood.* New York: Ballantine Books, 1974.

HUMPHREY, CLIFFORD C., Director, *Ecology Action Education Institute*, Box 3895, Modesto, Cal. 95352.

JACKSON, PHILIP. *Life In Classrooms*. New York: Holt, Rinehart and Winston, 1968.

JOHNSON, LELAND. *Bioenergetics*. Houston, Tex.: Espiritu Institute, 1974.

JUNG, CARL G. *Psychological Types*. Trans. H. G. Baynes. New York: Harcourt Brace, 1923.

———. *Psychology and Religion*. New Haven, Conn.: Yale University Press, 1938.

LA CHAPELLE, DOLORES, and JANET BOURQUE. *Earth Festivals*. Silverton, Col.: Finn Hills Arts, Publishers, 1974.

LEONARD, GEORGE B. *The Transformation*. New York: Dell Publishing Co., Inc., 1972.

———. *The Ultimate Athlete*. New York: Avon Books, 1977.

LE SHAN, LAWRENCE. *The Medium, The Mystic and The Physicist*. New York: Ballantine Books, 1975.

LUFT, JOE. *Of Human Interaction*. Palo Alto, Cal.: National Press, 1969.

MANN, JOHN, and HERBERT A. OTTO. *Ways of Growth*. New York: Grossman Publishers, 1968.

MARTIN, R., and A. KELLER. *Teacher Awareness of Classroom Dyadic Interactions*. Paper presented at American Educational Research Association annual meeting, Chicago 1974.

MASLOW, ABRAHAM. *Toward a Psychology of Being*. New York: Van Nostrand, 1968.

MAY, ROLLO. *Power and Innocence*. New York: Dell Publishing Co., Inc., 1972.

MISHLOVE, JEFFREY. *The Roots of Consciousness*. New York: Random House, Inc., 1975.

NEWBERG, NORMAN, and TERRY BORTON. In *Affective Education Development Research Report*. Ed. W. Gollub. Philadelphia, Pa.: Philadelphia School District, 1971.

NYQUIST, EWALD B., and GENE R. HAWES. *Open Education*. New York: Bantam Books, 1972.

ORNSTEIN, ROBERT E. *The Psychology of Consciousness*. San Francisco: W. H. Freeman, 1972.

ORR, LEONARD and SONDRA RAY. *Rebirthing in the New Age*. Millbrae, Cal.: Celestial Arts, 1977.

OTTO, HERBERT A. *Group Methods to Actualize Human Potential*. Beverly Hills, Cal.: The Holistic Press, 1970.

PEARCE, JOSEPH CHILTON. *The Crack in the Cosmic Egg*. New York: Pocket Books, 1971.

————. *The Magical Child.* New York: E. P. Dutton, 1977.

PELLETIER, KENNETH R., and CHARLES GARFIELD. *Consciousness: East and West.* New York: Harper & Row, Publishers, 1976.

PETERMAN, DAN J. "Toward Interpersonal Fulfillment in an Eupsychian Culture." *The Journal of Humanistic Psychology*, 12, No. 1 (Spring 1972), 72–85.

PROGOFF, IRA. *At A Journal Workshop.* New York: Dialogue House Library, 1975.

RATHS, LOUIS, MERRILL HARMON, and SIDNEY SIMON. *Values and Teaching.* Columbus, Ohio: Charles E. Merrill, 1966.

RING, KENNETH. "A Transpersonal View of Consciousness: A Mapping of Farther Regions of Inner Space." *The Journal of Transpersonal Psychology*, 6, No. 2 (1974), 125–55.

ROZMAN, DEBORAH. *Meditating With Children.* Boulder Creek, Cal.: University of the Trees Press, 1975.

SAMPLES, ROBERT. "Mind Cycles and Learning." *Phi Delta Kappan*, 59, No. 5 (1977), 688–92.

SCHUL, BILL, and ED PETTIT. *The Psychic Power of Pyramids.* Greenwich, Conn.: Fawcett Publications, Inc., 1976.

SIMON, SIDNEY B., LELAND W. HOWE, and HOWARD KIRSCHENBAUM. *Values Clarification.* New York: Hart Publishing Company, Inc., 1972.

SPRINTHALL, RICHARD C. and NORMAN A. SPRINTHALL. *Educational Psychology: A Developmental Approach.* Menlo Park, Cal.: Addison-Wesley Publishing Company, 1974.

STEINER, CLAUDE. *Scripts People Live.* New York: Grove Press, 1974.

TOFFLER, ALVIN. *Future Shock.* New York: Bantam Books, 1970.

————. *Learning for Tomorrow.* New York: Vintage Books, 1974.

VAN DUSEN, WILSON. *The Natural Depth in Man.* New York: Harper & Row Publishers, Inc., 1972.

WALKER, EUGENE C. *Learn to Relax.* Englewood Cliffs, N.J.: Prentice-Hall, Inc., 1975.

WATTS, ALAN. *The Book on the Taboo Against Knowing Who You Are.* New York: Macmillan Publishing Co., 1968.

WEINHOLD, BARRY K. "Restoring Natural Power, A Manual for Counselors." Unpublished work, 1978.

WEINHOLD, BARRY K., and GAIL ANDRESEN. *Threads: Unraveling the Mysteries of Adult Life.* New York: Richard Marek, Publishers, 1979.

WEINSTEIN, GERALD, and MARIO D. FANTINI, eds. *Toward Humanistic Education.* New York: Praeger Publishers, 1970.

Index